Preface

The history of Black women in America is one in which there has been much joy and a lot of pain. It is not easy being a woman in this society, particularly a Black woman because we suffer from the triple burden of race, class and gender. We have three strikes against us: we are women, strike one. We belong to a class that is associated with poverty and welfare, strike two. And most importantly, we are Black, strike three. That is the ultimate strike, the solidifying thread that entangles us in a society that was not created for us.

Negative stereotypes about Black women are abundant and have been used to keep us in our place as the dregs of American culture. Hood-rat, gold-digger, welfare queen, crack whore, video whore are the new labels and Sapphire, Mammy, and Jezebel are the older ones. But Black women are much more than these labels. We are mothers, wives, lawyers, teachers, doctors, preachers. We juggled work and family life long before it became the norm, neglecting our health to keep our children fed, clothed and sheltered. Black women in America are among its most unique citizens. We have survived the horrors and degradations of slavery, the failure of Reconstruction and the dehumanization of Jim Crow/segregation and still we rise. Our stories need to be told.

This anthology consists of blogs I have written in the past year and consists of a collection of non-fiction and fiction essays about being Black and female in America. Some of these stories are funny. Some are so sad that you can almost taste the salt of the tears that have flowed. But these stories are necessary because in order to move forward, you need to look within.

Ghetto Nation

Ghetto - A section of a city to which an entire ethnic or economically depressed group is restricted; as by poverty or social pressure.

Life for blacks who reside in the inner-city has never been easy but in the years since crack cocaine hit, things have most definitely taken a turn for the worst. A new breed of black woman and manhood has arisen and they behave rather badly. It has become absolutely normal to be ignorant and ghetto and more scarily, this behavior is celebrated with glee.
Take a stroll in any inner-city neighborhood: On any given afternoon, you will see groups of able-bodied young men lounging carelessly on street corners, smoking marijuana boldly on street corners bragging about their bitches, whores and baby mammas. Although these young men show clear shiftless tendencies, throngs of ride or die chicks, sometimes with several children in tow surround them, taking loudly while dressed in pajama bottoms and dingy white wife-beaters complete with the proverbial head scarf.

These words are not stereotypes but actual truth. Too many times, blacks complain about their dirty laundry being aired publicly instead of fixing the problem and it is time to discuss an issue that is plaguing us as a people: the acceptance of ignorance. Although racism is, has been, and will always be a part of American society, social behaviors once deemed deviant are embraced and accepted by some blacks.

Urban terrorists have hijacked urban communities throughout America, but calling the police is considered "snitching" and murderers walk around unafraid and unrepentant. Mothers hide the guns of their gang-banging sons and little children are left at home unattended with an empty refrigerator while their parents party in the streets. There are so many examples of this behavior that I could go and on but that would be redundant. However, one thing rings true, regardless if some folks do not want to face it: gutter, hood-related anti-social behavior is running amok in some black communities.

Where did it all go so terribly wrong? The decline of the inner-city black family can be traced to the crack cocaine era. Black families throughout America were decimated due to drug abuse and drug dealing and the children became collateral damages. An entire generation of Black children has grown up seeing their parents either use or sell drugs and it has destroyed their psyche.

For these young adults, the only thing worth living for is the mass consumption of expensive designer clothing, alcohol, drugs and sexual escapades with multiple partners. They have no goals or ambitions but to live for the day. An education is scorned as being nothing more than a worthless piece of paper and disputes are settled by gunfire, regardless of who is around.

The blame for this generation of inner-city hoodrats can be laid at the feet of Black Generation X, my generation. Blacks born between 1965 and 1976 were the first recipients of the gains that the Civil Rights Movement had battled for and we squandered it by getting caught up in the "Greed is Good" era of the Eighties. We ran the streets instead of taking care of our children, shoving the responsibility of childrearing on our weary, overworked parents. We were more concerned about outer appearances, spending money on a bunch of stuff instead of saving money for better educational opportunities and now our children still lag behind every ethnic group when it comes to reading, writing, and arithmetic. Instead of being parents to our children, we became their friends, smoking blunts with them and allowing their boyfriends and girlfriends overnight privileges, creating the next generation of out of wedlock children.

We planted the seeds for mass destruction and now we have a garden full of weeds. It saddens me to write this but it is my opinion that little can be done to correct this hood-related behavior. These days, you cannot tell anyone anything bad about their children because it might cause a physical confrontation. The US government could put trillions of dollars into every inner-city in America but this ghetto mentality will still exist because being absolutely nothing is accepted. An entire generation of black young adults has accepted their caste in society as the lowest of the low, trapped by the narrow confines of their minds and neighborhoods.

A Letter to My Molester – Inmate K53771 Jimmie L. Hunt

Lawrence Correctional Center
10930 Lawrence Road
Sumner, Il 62466

Dear Mr. Hunt:
This letter to you has been a long time coming. If you don't remember me, my name is Kathy Henry, your ex-girlfriend Gertrude's daughter. You came into my life when I was ten-years-old and from the moment you appeared, I knew you were not shit. My mother thought that I was just jealous because I never had to share her before, but instinctively, I knew that your presence would mean no good for me.

At first, you seemed to be a good man for my mother. You helped pay her bills, gave me an allowance and pretended that you were a stand-up guy and father figure but you weren't. You were and still are a child molesting motherfucking pig who took away my innocence when I was eleven-years-old.
Do you remember coming into my bedroom when my mother was sleep and feeling on my then budding body? I used to lie in bed, fearing when you would come over because that meant I would have to sleep in my street clothes instead of a nightgown to protect myself. No little girl should have to go through that but that was my life for four years. Four fucking years.

You never penetrated me vaginally but the damage you inflicted on my psyche was immeasurable. I was just a little girl whose only thoughts were of Barbie Dolls, books and my cat Boogie-Woogie and you made me feel like a filthy whore because the feelings you stirred in my body felt good. How could a good girl act like that? From then on, I believed that I was no good and I blame you for that.

I became sexually active at the age of fifteen and was the mother to two children by time I was twenty-one-years old. No one put a gun to my head but you made feel like used goods and for a long time I believed that no decent man would want a nasty, dirty female like myself who got herself molested because I was wearing a size 38 Double D bra at the age of eleven.

I never told my mother you molested me because I was afraid that she would not believe me. I only told her after you got arrested for taking away the innocence of another little girl, age six and the pain in my mother's face is something that will haunt me until my dying day.

You are scheduled to be paroled on July 21, 2011, nine days before your 78th birthday but if I have my way, you will never get out because I plan on doing everything in my power to make sure your slimy ass stay behind bars for the rest of your life. You do not deserve to be on the street to have another opportunity to ruin another little girl's life. God knows how many little girls you molested but as long as I have breath in my body, you will never walk the streets of Chicago again.

It is not fair that you are alive to see another birthday and my mother is dead. She died five years ago from complications from diabetes and I still mourn her passing everyday. But the world we live in is not fair. She is in a better place and not in pain but you have been in pain everyday. No freedom, referred to as a number, no normal sex life. Oh, I forgot, you are not a normal man anyway but a fucking pervert.

I hope that the last fifteen years of your life has been hell on earth and that you are getting molested by some big, burly dude on a nightly basis. Child molesters get treated like shit in prison and I know that you have received your comeuppance. Do you lie on your bunk at night, scared and shaking, hearing the footsteps of your predator, knowing what is going to happen? Good.

Just one more question and I will leave you alone Mr. Hunt. How could you destroy my life so willfully? I was a little girl and with one act, you took away my innocence and my ability to ever trust a man fully. I have come to the conclusion at the age of forty that I will probably never get married because I do not have it in me to give myself totally in a relationship because I do not trust men.

In a just society, you would have been sentenced to life in prison for your crimes, but unfortunately, that is not the way of the American judicial system. Maybe you have repented but I doubt it. A leopard doesn't change his spots but learns to camouflage. God may have mercy on your soul but I do not and I hope that you rot in hell.

Sincerely,

Kathy M. Henry

Freestyle Ramblings

I am a writer who does not write as much as I should. I have some talent but I do not have the passion that is truly necessary to be a writer because most of my passion is being used to find employment. It's hard being a writer and you are broke as hell. I need money and in this society, you don't work, you don't eat. I am trying to make it by way of my wits, so when I finally decide to write, I write about things that are bothering me. Like the economy. Like the fact that myself and millions of other Americans are either unemployed or underemployed. The powers that be and the corporate media are trying to bamboozle the American public into believing that everything economical is okey-dokey and our broke asses should run to the malls immediately and spend, spend, spend on overpriced, tacky looking junk.

The Republicans swept into power in November by pretending that they were really concerned about the millions of Americans who were spit on by the Great Depression of 2007 and Beyond and would put them back to work. Full of hubris and glee, they shouted to the rooftops that the American people had spoken and swore that they would do their duty by them. However, once in, they took their suits off and reverted back to their native snake skins and proceeded to enforce their perceptions of reality on everybody else by attempting to take funding away from Planned Parenthood, trying to redefine rape as "forcible", and slashing the hell out of programs that assist the poor such as WIC, early childhood education, heating assistance and any other crumbs that poor folks had managed to lick off the floor after the masters ate.

I mentioned the poor instead of middle-class because the very term "middle-class" has become archaic in America society. If you have to work because the money you make will pay your bills in order to live, then you are poor. If you survive off your job, good credit and credit cards and happen to lose your job, your credit score dipped due to missing payments and you could not find employment, would you be okay financially? If no, you are poor and stop pretending otherwise. The concept of being middle-classed was merely an illusion perpetrated by the media, credit cards companies and several mortgages on homes that have since lost its value. But as usual I digress and please forgive me.

Although economic times are dark and dreary for the average individual, to my surprise and delight, after several years of suffering silently, some members of the American public have decided to fight against the powers that be and shut shit down. Public sector workers in Wisconsin have revolted against the government by protesting in the thousands against legislation that would take away nearly all collective bargaining rights from most public employees in the state. It feels good to see people in my country stand up for their rights, even though these people are being made out to be greedy, trifling, individuals who are sucking off the Great Government Tit at the taxpayers' expense by certain media outlets and politicians. The sad part about this is that some people actually believe this nonsense and are attacking unions, blaming unions for the demise of American society.

It is amazing how gullible and ignorant of American history some Americans are. Unions were responsible for the 40 hour work week, abolishing child labor, and making working conditions safe for ALL Americans, not just those who are in unions. I guess Karl Marx was right: According to false consciousness, a concept associated with Marx, people can be misled by the dominant ideology (the common set of beliefs and values taken for granted in their society) to act or think in ways contrary to their best interests without necessarily even realizing it. It happens all the time here in America and it is pathetic. As long as the corporate masters are able to afford their mansions and give out an occasional crust of bread, some of us are content to live in hovels and sprout rhetoric straight from Fox News. But some of us have waken up and decided to fight back.

Homophobia in the Black Community

The black community is filled with hypocrisy. Recently, I had a raging debate about gay marriage with a friend of mine who is a Christian and holier than thou. He feels that gays should be put on an island somewhere away from the God-fearing, good, self-righteous heterosexuals and compared homosexuality to bestiality and pedophilia, which is the silliest shit ever since it is illegal to have sex with children and animals. He also called me a bleeding heart liberal who unless I repent my evil, wicked ways is going to hell.

My counter argument was that marriage is a basic civil right that should not be denied based on sexual orientation and that blacks who are homophobic need to be ashamed for aligning themselves with bigotry. I also reminded him that I was already doomed for hell since my mother was not married when she gave birth to me and according to Deuteronomy 23:2 "A bastard shall not enter in to the congregation of the Lord; even to his tenth generation shall he not enter into the congregation of the Lord."

Naturally, he took offense at my words and hung up the phone. However, that backwards, overtly religious thinking about homosexuality in the African American community is one of our many problems. Many blacks become automatic Christians when it comes to equal rights for gays while ignoring the many social ills that are plaguing our people.

The Black church has jumped on the homophobia bandwagon full throttle. It is always nice to have someone to feel superior to, especially if you are not that superior yourself. And it is certainly a great way to get into the power and money racket—the gays are gonna get you and destroy everything you love—the same rhetoric that White conservative Christians have been using for decades. Why should only White people get to tap into that? Eddie Long, anyone?

And it is certainly a great deal easier to rage against the gay community than doing something about the fact that in the African American community 70% children are born out of wedlock compared to the rest of America. Our children are growing up without fathers and running amok without any guidance but the Black church do not want to talk about that. Our communities are plagued with rampant unemployment, drug and alcohol abuse, crime, and poverty but these issues are ignored because it is so much easier for all concerned to beat up on gay people.

What is truly sad is that marriage equality would totally benefit the black family. Stable gay couples would get married and hopefully adopt black children, considered the least desirable in the adoption world, the same ones who linger in the foster care system until they age out because of the sexual irresponsibility of black heterosexuals. There would be fewer men on the down low trying to prove they are not gay by fathering children they have no interest in raising or financially supporting. God help my people because it is a sad day in black history when it is more acceptable for a man to have ten children by ten different women than it is for him to be gay.

And I'm Ignorant – The Education System in America

The role that the educational system should play in the live of individuals is to educate them to be conscious, critically thinking individuals who do not passively accept knowledge but question the knowledge that is being taught to them. Education should be taught to give students the skills and intelligence they need to understand the world and how it works in order to survive in it.

However, the American educational system has been known to produce students whom are woefully ignorant about the history of America and different cultures. One of the reasons for this dilemma is because the educational system in its current state does not leave much room for critical thinking but trains individuals to be docile, worker bees in a decaying economy that keeps corporations wealthy and its workers barely making it.

The problem becomes evident if one looks at the varied curriculums and subjects that are being taught in the public schools. There is a lack of emphasis on academic learning, and the only thing that matters is high stakes testing. The schools in America have become swamped with fuzzy curriculums that assume that through constant testing, students will be prepared for life in a new global society . . . whatever that is.

In order for the educational system in this country to produce students who are not clueless about its history and the world surrounding them, it should be restructured in several ways. Parental involvement should be mandatory, just as school attendance for students is mandatory for graduation. Lack of parent involvement is an enormous contributing factor to the current failing educational system. Parents need to instill in their children the belief that an education is necessary, just like food, water, and shelter. Teachers are wonderful people who can take students from the top of Mount Olympus to the cold and desolation of Antarctica but they are there to teach, not parent. Many teachers spend a great deal of their class time disciplining children and playing babysitter, two things that are not a part of their job duties. Teachers need involvement from parents in order for the educational system to work and education begins at home.

Funding for the educational system should also be restructured. Public schools are traditionally funded by property taxes which is disastrous for poor neighborhoods. Communities that are wealthy have more funding for their local schools than those who do not. This situation directly affects the quality of education children in urban and poor rural areas receive. The No Child Left Behind Act has only made this situation worse because of the required testing and public reporting of results. When parents are buying a new house, they want to live in a school district that has strong test scores. This drives up the property values in those areas, meaning that only affluent families can afford to live in the top performing school districts. This means more funding for those areas, while the lower performing schools lose their funding if they do not meet federal standards.

There should be a fair tax system for education that is not based on the property taxes of homeowners. Government funding, for the most part, is distributed to the various schools by state and local governments and there is huge disparities in this funding based on race. According to Spring (2001), "There is a gap of more than $1,000 per student nation wide based on race in large states such as New York, Illinois, and Pennsylvania, who lead the nation in their unwillingness to fairly fund education" (pg. 77).

Children should not suffer because of their economic background or ethnicity and public education should make no distinctions between rich and poor, black and white. Every child attending a public school should be granted an equal education. Equal funding would give teachers the proper resources to better educate students. School choice and the privatization of the public school system would not be a factor because under this plan, the educational system in America would be fully and equally funded by the federal government and closely monitored. With the influx of money pouring into the educational system from the government, schools would change dramatically for the better because that is the biggest issue in most public schools is lack of money.

The educational system's curriculum would be changed in order to fit in with the nation's melting pot of different cultures and ethnicities. From elementary to high school, students are bombarded with facts and figures about wealthy, old white men as if women and other minorities do not exist or have contributed anything worthy to the history of America. No wonder so many students blank out historical facts: they do not care these facts because they cannot relate to the actors in the story. Student should be required to take courses that will give them a more in depth understanding of the world surrounding them, courses that will discuss the history of marginalized and oppressed individuals in this country and around the world. They should be required to read books that make them think, not just process information for the next test.

If more students understood the values and cultures of people unlike themselves, it would not be easy or maybe even impossible for the government and the media to use propaganda and lies to sway public opinion. High stakes testing would be eliminated because most of the tests given to students are designed by people who do not have a clue about the demographics, ethnicities or economic backgrounds of the students who are to be tested and these tests are biased against minorities and the poor. If students are to be tested, extra tutoring would be available to students, at no cost to the parents.

Having competent teachers, board members, and administrators are also a vital part of restructuring the educational system. What are the exact qualifications for an administrator or a board member? What type of degrees must they have? These are the questions that need answers and not just rhetoric. Board members should not be chosen because their personal relationship with the local mayor; all board members would have a Master's degree in Education or have an extensive background in social justice. As for the teachers, the educational system should make sure that the best teachers are chosen for the positions and evaluations should be given frequently.

This would give parents and the educational system a chance to find out what is wrong and what is needed to correct the problems. Public education needs teachers and board members who actually care about the children and their education, not individuals who want the perks of working for the school system: summers and holidays off, steady raises and a fat compensation package. American children are suffering due to the inadequacies of the individuals involved with the educational system.

The "culture of poverty" theory that has been used by several politicians to explain differences in learning between different ethnicities would be exposed as a blatant attempt by the status quo to "blame" individuals for their poverty. Huge educational gaps between poor students and wealthy students do not occur because the poorer students have adapted to their poverty-stricken existence but because they do not have resources necessary to succeed in school. If students have to deal with textbooks that are outdated, lack of toiletries, and computers from the late 1980s, and teachers who do not care about them, their opportunities for academic achievement is dismal and their chances of dropping out of school likely.

In a just and an equal society, the educational system discussed would have already been implemented decades ago but it has not and more than likely will not be implemented. In a hierarchical society such as in America, there will always be someone on the low end of the totem pole and the best way to do that is through the miseducation of its most vulnerable citizens: the children. The neglect of the educational system in the US threatens the economic well being of the entire nation. Unless the inequalities in education are diminished and its system totally restructured, the wealth gap between the rich and the poor will continue to widen and the US will be infamous for being the nation of the ignorant and undereducated.

Living in a Garbage Can

For the past two years and two months, I have resided in a garbage can. The smells of old garbage, urine, and human funk permeate the air of my surroundings, and stray cats yowl in the middle of the night. The garbage can where I live actually has a name and it is Parkway Gardens Apartments, a federally subsidized low-income housing unit on the South Side of Chicago.

How did a college educated individual like me end up living in a garbage can? After getting laid-off in August of 2007 from my job as an administrative assistant, it seemed like the Furies of Greek mythology was after me. Other than temp work, I could not find a job, full or part-time, and I could not afford the rent at my previous residence. I decided to look on the Department of Housing and Urban Development's (HUD) website for subsidized housing.

This is my second stint in subsidized housing. The first stint was from 2002 to 2007. During that time, I went to college, received a Bachelor's degree and maintained a 3.6 average, obtained a full-time job and my eldest daughter graduated from high school with a 4.2 grade point average, and then I moved. While receiving help from the government, a multitude of men did not live with me, nor did I have any more children, the stereotypical things that those poor, trifling black single mothers who receive government assistance are supposed to do. There is a concept amongst the common consensus that low-income housing is not supposed to be permanent, but rather a stepping stone to a better life and that is true. However, I did exactly what society told me to do (bettered myself and my children) and I almost ended up homeless. I was faced with the choice of residing in a shelter or Parkway Gardens, and I chose Parkway.

I have resided in some real flophouses during my lifetime but Parkway Gardens takes the cake. As a native South Sider, I have known about Parkway Gardens my entire life, but one has to live here to understand the madness that is Parkway. The stuff that goes on in Parkway is unbelievable considering that it is right down the street from the University of Chicago. Drug dealing, gang-banging, whoring; everything goes in Parkway Gardens! The filth is insidious and pervasive, the kind that follows you because no matter how hard you clean your apartment, the smell is there. At least it is to me. My son says that our apartment is fine but I am so paranoid, it is ridiculous.

But this story is not about me, but about how HUD is the biggest slumlord in the United States. There is no accountability for the owners of the properties that HUD gives monies to for rent payments. These owners are receiving millions of dollars from the government but put very little of said money into the general maintenance of the properties, leaving people to live in abject squalor at the taxpayers' expense.

I have called the multihousing unit hotline number that HUD has on its website several times to complain, but I was told that HUD has nothing to do with the upkeep; all they do is pay the rent. It is up to the owners and property management to take care of everything. I just want to know what stupid individual came up with the idea to take accountability from HUD and give it to the property owners who just want to make a buck.

The Tea Partiers and the Republicans are constantly carrying on about government waste and trying to slash Medicare and Medicaid, but they need to look into the budget for the Department of Housing and Urban Development because millions of dollars are going to waste. And by the way, Parkway Gardens Apartments has been sold to a real estate in New York for forty million dollars. Yes, forty million dollars for a 694 unit garbage can that houses over one thousand families. It is also rumored that Parkway makes over eight million dollars a year from rental subsidies all thanks to the largesse of HUD. Rather than looking for ways to cut and divert our attention to systems and programs that, while not always perfect, provide a benefit for the public good and well-being, politicians should actually take a closer examination at programs and systems (e.g. HUD) that need to either be amended or gentrified or the management carved and served in time for Thanksgiving.

My Take on Fantasia's Pregnancy Announcement

A couple of months ago, the blogosphere was in a tizzy about R&B singer, Fantasia's confirmation of pregnancy rumors. After cruising several websites and reading the comment section, the common consensus is that she is an ugly, stupid, uneducated hood rat who makes all Black women look bad. Angry or what? Too many folks out here are too harsh, hateful and judgmental of this woman's life and situation. I guess all of you are perfect, huh?

First of all, Fantasia is a grown-ass woman who has the financial means to take of a child and if she wants to pop out a baby every year, that is her business. According to her own words, she had previously had an abortion and she probably did not want to go through that experience again. She made the decision to bring life into the world and she has to live with this decision, not us.

Black women on these websites were her worst detractors, fearing that society will judge them because of Fantasia's actions. Guess what? American society has been judging us ever since we were brought here against our will to be workers and breeders. Nothing we do will ever satisfy society, Black or White so you have to live your life for yourself and be happy. A black woman is currently one of the most educated and intelligent First Ladies ever but she gets constantly attacked for her looks, her clothes, for having the nerve to be First Lady. So please get off your soap boxes and practice what you preach. Considering that 70% of black children are born out of wedlock, any sister who is sitting back judging Fantasia needs her ass whipped.

In regards to the father of the child, that is between him, Fantasia, his wife and the Lord. I am not any position to judge her because I am not a saint. But obviously there are a lot of saints in America because poor Fantasia has taken a beating on the Internet. People kills me with this judgmental shit, sitting back talking about another person as if they are the most perfect individuals on the planet. Does she not care for her current child? Are most children in this society planned? Hell no and these assumptions are truly misguided.

It just proves a theory of mine that most Americans are miserable as hell. Their own lives are so empty that they have to tear someone else down in order to feel good about themselves and that is pathetic. Let Fantasia have her baby in peace and stop judging so much. To be angry and filled with misery is not a good thing and be careful about looking down your nose at someone else: one day you may just find that you are looking back at yourself.

There Are No Daddies Here: The Consequences of Growing Up Fatherless & Female

Until several years ago, I had never put the correlation between growing up without a father and my past life experiences. When I was young, I was foolish enough to believe that not having a father was a good thing: it was one less problem I had to deal with or so I thought. I believed this nonsense until I read a great book by a wonderful author named Benilde Little. The name of the book is called The Itch, and it is the story of a woman who from the outside looking in, had the perfect life. She had a great husband, both had well paying careers, a beautiful home in the suburbs, and they were trying to have a baby. She thought everything was fine until her husband left her for a model and her perfect life crumbled. In her quest for self-discovery, she finally acknowledged that because she grew up without a father, she was constantly looking for a father figure. She put her husband on pedestal and made him a god. She wanted to please him so he wouldn't leave her like her father did, but in the end he did, and she wasn't surprised; deep down, she knew he would. She was playing out her childhood pain. Until she embraced her pain, she would never be free.

When I read this book for the first time, I cried. It was my story and it is always scary to acknowledge the truth. My significant other of eight years had left me and I was still foolishly waiting for him to come back. When I met him, I had two children, and he accepted them as his own. I felt so lucky to have a man like this that I put him on pedestal and put up with his infidelity, insensitivity towards my feelings and a whole lot of crap. I wanted the white picket fence lifestyle for my children and he was my chance for this; I did not want to let him go. Even when he left, I was still stuck on stupid, not realizing that even though he was committed to the children, he was not committed to me. I realize now that I needed the first man in my life to show me what I needed to look for in a good man. However, that was impossible. My father has been gone out of my life for so long; I can barely remember his face.

I never really knew my father. I was the result of an affair he and mother had when he was married; as a result I had limited opportunities to spend time with him. When I was four, their relationship ended and I did not see him again until I was twenty-four. My mother eventually got involved in another relationship when I was ten years old with a man I will call Pete. I never liked him and when I expressed his to my mother, she shrugged it off, saying I was jealous because I never had to share her before. That was true but he was always trying to kiss me and that made me feel uncomfortable. My worst nightmare came true when I was eleven when he started coming to bedroom late at night when my mother was sleep, fondling me all over my body and kissing me as he would a grown woman. This behavior continued until I was fifteen years old. He never penetrated me but the psychological damaged was done.

I always blamed myself for his actions because I matured physically early and had large breasts. If I did not have those things, this would have never happened to me. If I was truly a good girl, he would have never molested me. I never told my mother because of the way she blew me off when I told her I did not like him and I was afraid she would not believe me. He was generous financially, giving me an allowance and paying my mother's bills. I thought if I told her what happened, she would be angry with me for messing up her relationship with this "nice" man. She was employed a cook and almost everyday she would come home from work with burns on her arms. She was doing this type of work to support me and I could not rock the boat.

For many years, I felt like used goods because not only did my father abandoned me, I had to deal with illegitimacy issue. I had an aunt who used to do nice things for me such as buying school clothes, book supplies and keeping my hair done. Some of my cousins were jealous because of the attention I received from her, and one of them told me that her mother (my other aunt) told her the reason why Aunt Rosie did so many nice things for me is because I did not have a father and they did. That kind of talk can hurt a kid and it hurt me.

I eventually told my mother about that bastard Jimmie but that was only after when he was arrested for the rape of a six year old girl and he is currently serving a fifteen year sentence for that crime and is eligible for parole in 2016. I will be in court to stop that bullshit. I only wished I had had the strength at the time to tell someone what he had done to me. Maybe I could have saved that little girl a lifetime of grief and misery. God knows how many other little girls' lives he has ruined but the slimy motherfucker is locked up and I hope someone is molesting him.

My poor mother was so hurt when I told her truth and I hope I did not take years off her life. She told me she would have killed him if she had known. I am truly sorry that I did not have enough faith in our relationship to trust her but that is water under bridge.

When I think about the molestation and my father abandoning me, I am filled with so much anger and hurt, it scares me and for years, I blocked it out. How can a man leave his child to fend for herself in such a harsh, cruel world? How could my father leave me as if I was trash on the street? I wonder does he think about me and the fact that I turned forty-one this month and he has not done a damn thing for me. He has three beautiful grandchildren he has never seen and I wonder how he can live with himself for abandoning us.

As a little girl, I never had the pleasure of having my father kiss me goodnight and tell me bedtime stories. I grew up without having the most special man in a young girl's life, the one who loves you unconditionally, even if you get fat and pimply. I had to struggle alone with a father and make my way through life without having this type of security. I never knew what it was like to feel safe and secure in a father's love and that is a bitter pill to swallow. According to research, almost forty percent of the children in America will go to bed without their fathers in their lives, just as I did. I hope that their fathers will get themselves together before it is too late to help their children.

A Blacks Girl's Tale of Woe: Living without a Booty in a Bootylicious Society

It is a common misconception in American culture that every black woman has a big butt but that is not true. Since I turned forty last, I have been letting the bullshit go and it is time for me to come clean with something that has bothered me my entire life: I do not have a big butt. Furthermore, not having a big butt affected my self-esteem for many years and made me believe I was ugly. I never would have thought I would admit this truth about myself, but at my age, it is time to cut the bullshit and keep it real.

You see, when a woman thinks she is ugly, she has a tendency to make stupid mistakes like looking for love in all the wrong places, putting up with relationships that are going nowhere fast and generally taking a lot of shit off men who aren't good enough to wipe your ass. Lord knows I put up with some crappy relationships because of self-esteem issues but the greatest thing about growing older is the wisdom that comes with age. Never again will I let my life revolve around keeping a man happy at the expense of my own happiness. But I digress. Let me begin my tale.

Coming of age in the eighties was rough on young black women who didn't have big butts and I know because I was one of them. I have enormous boobs but black men don't put women who have large breasts on a pedestal like they do women with big butts. A woman can look like Medusa but if she has an enormous ass, she is given an automatic pretty pass regardless of how fucked up her face is. I know this girl who all the men loved and thought was so fine because she had a big booty. But her grill was jacked, she had horrible skin and she was not cute. Period point blank. I am not trying to be a hater but it irked me then and it irks me now when men carry on and on and on about a woman because her ass is big but her face is average at best. It is an insult to all the truly gorgeous black women out here who do not have big butts. We count too.

Everywhere I turned, music videos and raps songs glorifying the magnificence of the big booty were everywhere. A man even told me that all I had was big titties and no ass with much venom in his tone and I felt less than a cockroach. Some might say that I am exaggerating, but this mentality really exists in my community. When biker shorts came into vogue, I only brought one pair because more than one pair was a waste of time and money. Not having a big butt gnawed at me and during this period in my life, my self-esteem was officially in the gutter and I did so much stupid shit, it was pathetic. Sleeping with random men, drinking, doing drugs, I did it all, and it's by the grace of God that I am still alive to write this tale.

A weaker woman would have been broken by some of things I went through during my younger years but not me. Bent a little but never broken. But life is a continuing growing process, and over the years, I learned to love myself and all my imperfections, even my flat booty because this is the body type God meant for me to have. Most importantly, I came to this point in my life without the assistance of a man. I had to learn how to stand on my own feet and learn through the hard knocks of life that if I did not value myself, no man would value me, regardless of how big or small my ass was.

Eventually, I got myself together and I stopped worrying about how big my ass was and went back to school. I received my GED in 1997 and in 2002; I went to college and received a Bachelor's degree from Roosevelt University, graduating with a 3.6 grade point average while raising three children as a single mother in the hood. All by myself without any aid or assistance from a man and I feel good about that. That was the greatest validation I needed to know that I was somebody and not just for my body, but for my marvelous mind.

However, things have not changed in community about this issue. Sadly, although it's been over twenty years since my tale of woe, emphasis on a certain body part of black women is still prevalent, and if anything, it has gotten worse. Raps songs such as "She Got a Donk" by Souljah Boy is a club thumper and having a big booty can make an enterprising young woman a celebrity, except now young women who feel less than about the size of their booties can now buy the ass of their dreams. An upcoming, young female rapper has been rumored to have been injected with silicone to make her butt bigger and a ton of other shit in order to market herself as the Plastic Playmate of black men's wet dreams.

This mentality taken a toll on the self-esteem of black women everywhere who were blessed with the bodies God gave them and I hope my tale of woe helps them. We as black women need to reclaim our bodies from the chains of sexism that is running amok in the black community and love ourselves. Brothers need to recognize that beauty comes in all shapes and figures and limiting themselves to a certain body type will make them miss out on some great women. And everyone knows about that ironing board action. Best in the world!

To Weave or Not to Weave

For the past eighteen years of my life I have alternated between wearing my hair in its natural state and spending long hours in a beauty shop getting my hair chemically processed. When I first made the decision to go natural, my life was basically a mess: I had gotten struck by two cars (true story) and was in the hospital recuperating when I received a phone call telling my brother had died from a drug overdose in my bed.

My hair immediately started shedding from neglect and stress. One day while watching an Oprah episode about updating your look and how to stop dressing and living in the past, I looked in the mirror, picked up a pair of shears and rid myself of the few strands of chemically processed hair I had left attached to my head. I was finally free! Or was I? This was back in the 1994 when very few Black women in Chicago were wearing their hair in its natural status. I endured dirty looks, sniggers from women whose chemically processed hair was damaged and almost gone and generally a lot of negativity from my brainwashed Negro brethren.

During the summer of 1995, instead of ignoring the fools, I foolishly relaxed my hair on top of the blond dye I had put in my hair to camouflage my hereditary bald spots on the sides and guess what? My hair fell out on a nightly basis and I became bald as an egg. I had to go the local beauty supply shop to get a wig to cover up the mess that was my hair and start anew.

By the spring of 1996, I had gotten rid of the wig and was proudly sporting my afro. I was a queen and my afro was my crown. No one could tell me that I was not the most beautiful woman on the planet. Not the raggedly head women who gave me funny looks anytime I stepped on the bus. I pitied those women so brainwashed into believing their natural hair was so ugly that they would rather hang on to damaged, dry hair the texture of straw. Or wear cheap, tacky looking weave jobs so obviously fake that only a fool would be bamboozled into thinking that mess was real. I pitied the men who did not understand why I was wearing my hair natural and who tried to convince me to join the indoctrinated masses of Black women by relaxing my hair or wearing a weave.

However, by the spring of 1997, my attitude drastically changed. I had just completed a word processing class at the Chicago Urban League and was turned down for a receptionist position at that same prestigious organization by a light-skinned, long flowing hair older harridan because her issues about my hairstyle (Get rid of the afro because it makes me feel uncomfortable).

That attitude really hurt. Years of brainwashing has really done a number on the mentality of some Blacks and to be turned down for a job by my own people because of my hair, my own hair, my crown was a total kick in the ass. By the summertime, I decided to relax my hair once again because I needed a job and guess what? I received a job, not at the Chicago Urban League but somewhere else.

I kept this look for four years. From 1997 to 2001, I was at the beauty shop every Saturday from 7am until 5pm. I felt as though I was going to work. My children would look depressed because they knew they would not see their mother until later in the day and would call the shop to talk to me.

I have been thinking a lot about my hair and the issues I have dealt because this summer in the middle of a heat wave, I wore a wig (a hot ass wig) to a job interview and I still feel totally like crap considering I have not heard anything from the company. Thirty dollars down the drain to impress some people I will probably never meet again in this lifetime. Its enough that I have to put on my Happy Negro face and answer a bunch of dumb questions about my job experience and why would I be the best the person for the job.

One of these days, the next time I am asked this question on a job interview, I am going to reply, "Because I really need a fucking job. I have bills to pay, children to support, and I would be a great asset to your company because I have managed to keep all my bills paid without anything getting cut-off, paid for my son's graduation expenses and accomplished all of these without any financial assistance from anyone other than the unemployment benefits some people believe are being used to buy drugs and alcohol".

Of course I am not going to say this (maybe) but I am waiting for the day Martin Luther King Jr. spoke about so eloquently: "I have a dream that my four little children will one day live in a nation where they will not be judged by the color of their skin, but by the content of their character". Hopefully one day soon, my poor brainwashed Negroes will come from under the cloud of unawareness and learn to worship everything that comes with being Black. Any society that placed a skinny drug addict (Kate Moss) on the pedestal of beauty and femininity that all American women should aspire to is a society that is really twisted.

If I was White, Female and Privileged for One Day

First of all, before I write this essay, I would like to state that I love being a black woman. I love the beautiful brownness of my skin, my hair which is a crown that has anointed me Queen of my universe, my full lips, slanted eyes, and the strength of my ancestors who have dealt with much adversity during their journeys here in America and whose blood flow proudly in my veins. But I have to admit, I wonder what it would be like to be a white female just for a day to see what it would to be like to be considered Aphrodite rising from the sea because at times, it is hard being a black women in society that is sexist and has placed women who look like me on the bottom rung of every ladder in American society from economics to beauty.

White privilege is a critical race theory I came across in college during an African American history class. I had to read an article entitled, White Privilege: Unpacking the Invisible Knapsack by Peggy McIntosh and it opened my mind to some concepts I had never thought about before. According to this article, white privilege can be defined as unearned advantages enjoyed by white people beyond those commonly experienced by people of color in the same social, political, and economic spaces (nation, community, workplace, income, etc.) just because they are white.

White privilege is a topic some whites do not want to talk about because in admitting they are privileged because of their skin color would mean admitting that racism still exists and is not a pigment of black folks' imaginations but I digress. It must be nice living in a world where almost every image of your kind is thought to be good and pure and I would like some of that privilege just for one day.

Just for once, it would be nice to go on a job interview and not have to worry about the texture of my hair and wonder if the person I am interviewing with has a problem with afros, two-strand twists, or any other "black ethnic" hairstyle I might be wearing that day. If I was a white woman, I could toss my silky, long hair around with no problems.

Just for once, it would be nice not to be labeled an angry, bitter, black female who is filled with hatred just because I happen to have an opinion different from the black man that I am debating with. If I was white woman, I could be as argumentative as I want and be told that I am merely feisty. Black men would swim through a river of snot for me and tell me that black women are just too combative to be considered "wifey" material and that is why 40% of African American females remain unmarried. As a white woman, I would be able to date freely and not be told by my peers to lower my expectations or else die a lonely and miserable spinster with five kids with five different fathers.

Just for once, it would be nice to see someone who looks like me on a regular basis on the covers of high fashion magazines and playing the role of the leading lady in movies and television shows. As a black woman, I am constantly scolded by the media and some of my people for being too dark, too nappy, and too fat and that I will never be placed on that anointed pedestal as the standard of beauty and loveliness for American society. If I was a white woman, this problem would be null and void because I would be considered the crème de la crème.

But alas, I am a black woman and that is nothing to shirk at. The strength and tenacity of black women who can make something literally out of nothing is something to be admired than scorned and I am proud to be one. I actually feel sorry for white women sitting upon that fabled pedestal because it is a lonely tour of duty filled with unrealistic and shallow expectations and most fall swiftly and hard from that same pedestal. Better to be me with all my flaws, real and imagined than to be the poster child of impossible beauty. But I can keep it real; sometimes I wonder what it would be like to be a white woman. In my world, black women are called everything but a child of God and for once, it would be nice to be the anointed one.

City Within a City - Bronzeville

The Bronzeville neighborhood means so much to me because much of my family's history has been entwined in the area called Bronzeville, or as some call it, The Low End. My family started migrating from Mississippi during the 1940s. My Uncle Joseph was the first Allen to make the trek to the Promised Land and for him, the journey was bountiful. He started a Ma and Pa grocery store on 45th and Wabash with the help of his wife, my Aunt Edna, who worked as a laundress. With the proceeds of both their earnings, they purchased two buildings, including the one where his store was located. After that, the rest of my family, including my grandmother, with hope high in their hearts came to Chicago to make their fortunes. Some succeeded and some did not. However, that was not really important. What was important is that they had the opportunity to succeed, an opportunity that had been denied to them in their hometown of Itta Bena, Mississippi because of the rampant racism that existed. My own experiences with Bronzeville started in 1989, when my mother, my daughter and I moved to 49th and Prairie. We lived there until 1992, and in spite of what anyone says about that area, I had a ball. I had never seen such colorful characters that actually existed outside of books.

Bronzeville got its name because of the mass influx of African-Americans who came to Chicago that settled in the areas between 29th and 51st Street, during the Great Migration. Bronzeville was once a city within a city, with its own stores, several newspapers and strong churches. This neighborhood was dubbed the Black Metropolis because of all the opportunities offered to blacks. It became a magnet for African Americans, who were migrating from the South in droves. Jobs were plentiful and there were many black-owned businesses such as banks, insurance companies and funeral homes. There were many social institutions to help the disadvantaged and activities for people to immerse themselves in. The nightlife was fantastic. Musicians came from all over America to play at the Regal Theater and The Savoy. There were several blacks who lived in the Bronzeville area who became famous and they include: Ida B. Wells-Barnett, Ferdinand Barnett, Robert Abbott, Lionel Hampton, Richard Wright, Gwendolyn Brooks, George Cleveland Hall, T. K. Lawless, Jesse Binga, Anthony Overton, and Richard R. Wright. These African-Americans contributed many gifts that would stand the test of time.

However, in spite of its rich history, Bronzeville has faced a severe reversal of fortune. The losses of the stockyards and steel mills to different cities have pushed thousands of people out of the job market. Public housing projects - Stateway Gardens, Robert Taylor homes and the Ida B. Wells homes, created to give people better housing, trapped people in poverty and fear. The middle classed has moved to the suburbs. Retail businesses and lending capital have fled to safer pastures. This once proud Black Metropolis is now one of the poorest in the entire nation. The majority of its young people drop out of high school. Joblessness is the norm. Drugs and violence are rampant.

Even with all the adversity Bronzeville has faced in recent years, this community still has several strengths - beautiful old mansions, a great location near public transportation and the Loop, many churches, and a history so thick that you can feel it. This essay will be discussing two things that were very important to the Bronzeville area during its heyday: housing and religion. I will talk about the hard time black immigrants had getting decent housing due to overcrowding, segregation and what solution was taken to correct it, but ultimately caused a bigger problem. I will also discuss the religious wars that took place between the old guard blacks that had already settled in Chicago and the new immigrant blacks. There has been a great deal of renewed interest in the Bronzeville area because of its rich history, so hopefully, some of the money spent on other areas in the city of Chicago will be spent on this beautiful city within a city, the city called Bronzeville.

Results

The Great Migration forced the established African American community in Chicago to make major adjustments and accommodations for its new inhabitants. Historically, black churches had, like their counterparts in the South, resisted any involvement in social issues. The arrival of hundreds of thousands of migrants, however, simply could not be ignored and churches, being the black community's richest and most influential institution, were quickly called to action in the effort to help migrants properly adjust themselves to life in Chicago.

African Americans already living in Chicago were known as the Old Settlers and they were aware of the major implications the Great Migration would have on their lifestyle. The Old Settlers had striven to establish respect from whites and a sense of equality within the city's socioeconomic system. With the arrival of the Southern blacks, most of whom unfamiliar to city life, the Old Settlers feared that the progress they had achieved would be dashed. White people would probably equate them with the thousands of uneducated, fresh from the country migrants. Most importantly, the Old Settlers realized the enormous strain placed on many of the migrants who, having fled the South for better opportunities arrived in Chicago lacking housing or a sense of direction. From the migration's outset, African American Chicago area churches bore the brunt of the responsibility for helping guide the migrants.

The Old Settlers also worried that the temptations of Chicago's nightlife would be too much for the green as grass migrants. Down South, the church was the center of social life. Chicago, on the other hand, provided numerous outlets for entertainment (bars, nightclubs, taverns, gambling halls), many of them deemed by the ministry as deviant and destructive. African American social activist Richard Wright, Jr. emphasized the importance the church played in welcoming migrants to Chicago. He said, "Get these Negroes in your churches; make them welcome; don't turn your nose and let the saloon man and the gambler do all the welcoming. Help them buy homes, encourage them to send for their families and to put their children in school" (Sernett, Promised Land).

One of the first churches to help the immigrants was Olivet Baptist Church which is located on 31st and King Drive. This church assumed a major role in the process of aiding migrants. The Rev. Lacey Kirk Williams, the minister at that time, sent members of his church to several Chicago train terminals to meet incoming passengers. Church members greeted the newcomers and immediately directed them to places of assistance. Olivet quickly transformed itself into a social service center for migrants, providing them with food and clothing, while assisting them in the obtainment of housing and employment. They also hosted a wide variety of social, educational, and recreational activities, and soon gained a reputation throughout the South "as an oasis of mercy in the urban desert" (Sernett, Promised Land).

There would be major clashes between the migrants and the established Old Settlers, some of which concerned religion but most of which had to do with class status. The new migrants did not like the Northern churches. They felt that these churches were cold and impersonal. They were used to the expressiveness of the churches down South and to them; the Northern church services were restrained. The established Northern blacks felt that the new migrants were countrified and embarrassing. They liked the calmness of their church services and did not want change. They were also concerned about their own hierarchy in Chicago.

Some churches compromised their traditional religious practices in order to accommodate their new members. They incorporated gospel choirs, and added new, more vibrant songs to their traditional church hymns. Ministers livened up their sermons by interjecting "shouts" and encouraging emotional responses from the congregation. Still, the migrants still found themselves set apart by their class status, appearance and demeanor. The condescending attitudes toward the migrants by the predominately upper-class church congregations did not help the situation. They made fun of the migrants' clothes, accents, and lack of education. It always amazes me that in spite of all the racism and contempt we have endured from other cultures that we would treat each other so shabbily.

Some of these migrants eventually left these churches and started their own denominations. The churches came to be known as Storefront Churches. These churches tried to recreate the Southern rural churches that the majority of the migrants were used to. E. Franklin Franzier explained that the storefront churches "represented an attempt on the part of migrants, especially from the rural areas of the South, to re-establish a type of church to which they were accustomed" (Sernett, Promised Land).

Of course, the established black churches felt that these churches were a slap in their faces. They felt that these churches were a disgrace to the African American race and nothing more than a minstrel show. The preachers from these churches were derided for their lack of formal training and were subjected to accusations including defrauding their flock of money, being agents in the numbers racket, and of immoral sexual behavior (Sernett, Promised Land). Despite such criticisms, storefront churches persisted, and exist to this very day, their presence a testament to the strength of migrants' willingness to keep their Southern heritage and an unwillingness not to bow down to those who looked down their noses upon them.

The new migrants having settled the issue of religion now had to deal with housing. The majority of people lived in tenement housing and there were many horror stories about overcrowding, rats and insects. However, living conditions in Chicago, though overcrowded, were similar to housing conditions in the South. Down South, most migrants lived in three or four room cabins. It was not uncommon for as many as five people to sleep in one room.

But this was The Promised Land, and things were suppose to be better. As soon as they were able to get themselves together, they changed residences. Living conditions were used as a measure of the success or failure of migration. A family succeeded when they secured a place of their own.

One of the most popular living spaces for migrants was kitchenette apartments. These apartments were called that because everything was enclosed in one room, including the kitchen and are similar to what is called an efficiency apartment today, except a bit smaller and housing more people. Families of four and up lived in these small spaces. Many families took an apartment like this, dreaming of the day when a better life would come along.

I came to know this type of apartment very well. My mother, my then-baby daughter and I lived in a kitchenette apartment from 1989 to 1992. We had been burned out of our previous apartment and lost everything we owned. We needed to start off from scratch and save some money in the process. Unlike the migrants, we did have two separate rooms. The kitchen was actually pretty large and so was the bedroom/living space but we had to share a bathroom with the other tenants.

There was a pimp and his two ladies of night living down the hall, and they would fight everyday. Sometimes, the girls would fight each other and on other days, would join forces and beat up the pimp. A lady named Dorise lived across the hall and she would get drunk everyday. Her boyfriend was a drunk too, and one time when he was laid out across the lawn in a drunken stupor, someone stole his brand new Reebok gym shoes off his feet. When the first of the month came (check time), the tenants of 4949 South Prairie would party like it was New Year's Eve. It was truly an experience I will never forget.

By the 1940s, as more migrants flooded Bronzeville, there was less and less space for them to move into. Already decrepit apartments became overcrowded and the living conditions became worse. To alleviate this overcrowding, many blacks attempted to move to into neighboring areas and out to the newly emerging suburbs.

However, they were met with massive white resistance, both political and violent, forcing them to stay confined in the overcrowded and dilapidated slums of the South Side. The City of Chicago needed to do something about these conditions; there was a serious housing shortage and the migrants either did not have the money to move elsewhere, or could not because of white resistance. The Chicago Housing Authority, a government agency, attempted to solve the housing problems of the South Side by building affordable housing projects.

The first of these housing projects to finished were the Ida B. Wells Homes, and they were completed in 1941. The next to be finished were The Dearborn Homes, which are located from 27th to 30th streets and from State Street to the Rock Island Railroad tracks. They were completed in 1950. They were designed by Loebl, Schlossman and Bennet and represented the CHA's first "high-rise" public housing project. They ranged from 6 to 9 stories. The most notorious of the housing projects built by the CHA were The Robert Taylor Homes, Chicago's (and the country's) largest housing project. They were completed in 1962. They were named after Robert R. Taylor, the commissioner of the CHA from 1938-1950. Robert Taylor resigned from the CHA in 1950 after realizing that the political forces in Chicago would prevent the CHA from building unsegregated public housing. These political forces wanted blacks isolated and segregated from the rest of Chicago. And it worked.

The Robert Taylor Homes, consisting of 28 identical sixteen-story buildings practically guaranteed segregation because it was built in the middle of the slums of Bronzeville, keeping its over 28,000 residents isolated. By stacking people literally on top of each other, the CHA was able to house many people on this two-mile piece of land. The architects, who designed this madness, had hoped the open space surrounding the Robert Taylor Homes would give its residents a sense of closeness to the outdoors, making The Robert Taylor Homes suburbia within the city. However, the land surrounding the buildings served more as an isolating factor Because of its isolation, these projects became a hot seat of criminal activity, which included drug trafficking, gang wars and murder. Public housing, instead of giving the poor an outlet of hope, continued the vicious cycle of poverty and turned Bronzeville into a ghetto.

Conclusion

Bronzeville was once a bustling center of activity for African-Americans who wanted to better their lives. Once the jobs left the community, it took the heart out of Bronzeville. The projects took its soul. What is left now is an empty shell of broken beer bottles and shattered dreams. There has been a great deal of renewed interest in Bronzeville, and some of the old, abandoned buildings are being rehabbed. New businesses are coming back and putting money in the community.

If this interest continues, this neighborhood can be great again, but two key ingredients are needed to make this dream come true. The churches of Bronzeville have to take a more active role in the lives of its inhabitants, like they did in when the Migration first started. The ministers cannot turn a blind eye to the gang violence and drug activity that still plagues this area. The residents of Bronzeville also have to take a stand and not allow their neighborhood to continue its descent into the gutter.

The residents have to teach their children about Bronzeville's rich history. Bronzeville was built on the blood, sweat and tears of black migrants who came to Chicago with nothing in their pockets but dreams and a hope for the future. The children of Bronzeville should never be allowed to forget this. Bronzeville is the proverbial diamond in the rough. Let's hope its shine will come through.

The Importance of Knowing Your Heritage
Knowledge is like a garden: if it is not cultivated, it cannot be harvested - African Proverb

Up until nine years ago, I was very ignorant about my ethnic heritage. The only black history that was taught to me was during Black History Month. Even then, I only learned a part, not the whole. According to some of my grade and high school history textbooks, blacks were nothing more than savages whose only contributions to the world were farming and slaves.

Only when I went to college did I learn about the rich and interesting history that is my cultural birthright. Stories of women such as Ellen Craft, a slave who disguised herself as a white male while her husband pretended to be her servant in order to escape the chains of bondage. I was like a kid in a candy store. I had so much information and so little time to learn everything that had been hidden from me. I immediately became angry. Angry at the school system that had bamboozled me and so many other generations of black children. Angry at myself not seeking this knowledge sooner. But this anger was a good thing. I would never allow myself to be this ignorant again and I would make sure that my own children would know about their heritage, with or without the educational system's help.

However, there are many in the African-American community who are unaware of their heritage, other than what is shown on television. There are some who actually believe that stereotypical nonsense about Africans swinging in trees like monkeys when the slave boats came and that is so disheartening. The most tragic consequence of this mentality is that many African-American children are growing up today complacently ignorant about their heritage, not caring about anything other the latest pair of Air Jordans and the new hot rap single.

According to African-American historian John Henrik Clarke, in order to control a people, you must first control what they think about themselves and how they regard their history and culture. And when they feel ashamed of their culture and their history, prison chains are not necessary. This statement is a true assessment of what is going on in the black community. Many generations of African-Americans have been poisoned with self-hatred as a result years of slave mentality programming. Some of us have forgotten about the blood, sweat, and tears of Africans who were brought to this country against their will and whose blood still runs deeply in our veins.

That is why it is so important to know one's heritage. We have to break the cycle of complacent ignorance when it comes to our ethnic past. We know that the school system is not going to teach our children anything other than prepping for standardized state tests. We cannot let another generation of African-American children suffer from cultural degradation. In our veins, flow the blood of kings and queens who fought and died for their beliefs and who would be saddened by the state of their descendants who have forgotten where they come from.

The Racist Next Door

When most people think of racists, images of angry white men in white robes and hoods burning crosses in the yards of terrified blacks come to mind. However, since the advent of the Internet, a racist might actually be in the cubicle next to you at work or happen to be the person that will interview you for a job and that is a really scary thought.

Since the election of the first black President of the United States, racist rhetoric about minorities, particularly blacks posted online has risen to all time levels according to my own polling results. Anytime there is an article about crimes committed by black people posted on various websites such as the Suntimes.com or Yahoo, angry whites filled with fear and loathing spew all types of stereotypical nonsense. However, when a crime is committed by whites in a predominantly white area, one can almost hear the crickets chirping. Hell, it can be a positive story about minorities and some fool will write something ignorant in order to make their miserable lives better

Hispanics and Muslims have taken a beating online also. According to the unenlightened masses online, illegal Mexican immigrants are taking over America and Muslims cannot wait to bomb America to hell. Anybody other than white and Christian is suspect and will be tossed to the lions.

Most of this racist rhetoric is based on fear.

According to statistics, whites are going to be the minority in this country by 2042, so some whites are running around like foxes in the henhouse, worried about keeping their notions of white superiority intact. What these individuals do not understand is that they have nothing to fear. Institutionalized racism and notions of white superiority are deeply ingrained in American society and regardless of if whites do become the minority, nothing is going to change. In inner-cities throughout America, black youth are killing and shooting each daily and they are not concerned about white people. I cannot speak for other minorities but I would bet my last dollar that other minorities are not concerned about harming whites either.

What I fear most is in today's economic turndown, some of the best and brightest are going to be locked out of the job market due to their ethnicity and someone else's insecurity about changing demographics. It is hard enough trying to find a job without worrying about the color of your skin.

Sexism Run Amok, Amok, Amok

As a woman who lives in America, the land of the supposed free, it is always amazing to me that it is always men, who will never be pregnant or have to worry about the messy entanglement of a unwanted pregnancy (because they have the option of walking away), are always the main individuals who shout from the rooftops about how wrong abortion is and the rights of the unborn but do not want to give so much as one used food stamp for the survival of these babies.

Some of these men were foolishly elected to public office by uninformed and biased Americans who voted against their own economic and social interests and they are now trying to force their narrow viewpoints about female sexuality upon the American public by adding a rider to federal budget negotiations that are currently taking place that would abolish almost 300 million dollars in federal assistance to Planned Parenthood, an organization that helps low-income women with birth control, pap smears and abortion services and counseling (which is not free since it is illegal for the US government to fund abortions) and these negations have almost brought the American government to its knees.

Back story: The US government is facing a shutdown because of budget issues for 2011 as they work out a new budget. Both Republicans and Democrats have not come to an agreement due to the issue about Planned Parenthood, and this could cause the federal government to stop functioning on April 8, 2011, which is today!

Supposedly, negations are taking place to avert this madness, but the last major obstacle to compromise is defunding of Planned Parenthood. The US government is about to shut down because the pandering of certain politicians who are intent on catering to their ignorant, uneducated base who want women firmly entrenched in the kitchen, barefoot, uneducated, and pregnant without any choices.

In 2011, it is hard to believe that the culture wars are still alive and in full effect but unfortunately, it is true. Some people are still stupid enough to believe that if government assistance is taken away from Planned Parenthood, women will no longer have any options when it comes to abortion. It will be more expensive but if a woman does not want to continue a pregnancy, she will find a way to make it happen. These same people want to take society back the 1950s when everything supposedly was sunny and bright but thousands of women were miserable in suburbanite lifestyles and taking prescription drugs and blacks were water hosed and beaten for fighting for basic human rights.

It sickens me to see that our current elected officials are still on this nonsense during times of economic uncertainty. Will it ever be a time in which women will be able to control their own reproduction in America?

Middle-Age and Loving It!

In today's youth obsessed culture, believe or not, there are some perks to being an older woman. I turned forty last year and I have never felt freer. It sucks being a woman in a sexist society, particularly if you are a rebellious, free-thinking female like me who do not like to follow the litany of rules established for women. After trying to exist in this world made for men, I have been finally freed from the tired, worn out, patriarchal standards and regulations concerning women that have been in existence since time memorial because of my vast age. It seems to me, ever since I entered puberty, there was always some man trying to impose his narrow definition of women as they related to him upon me, whether I wanted his assistance or not and it totally pissed me off because of the arrogance of men who believe that because they have a penis, are naturally superior and smarter than women. Because I was young and naive, I did not have the courage to tell these men how I really felt but now, any man with this type of mentality can kiss my entire ass. It is a wonderful thing being pass forty because no one really gives a shit about older women because women over forty are considered passé, which means unlimited choices and freedoms. After many fruitless years of trying to fit in, I am able to be myself.

Collective Roots

Last year, I took my cat Diddy to get neutered, which was a very interesting experience. I went to the Lurie Spray/Neuter Clinic and it is located in the Little Village, a predominantly Mexican neighborhood I had never visited before, and for me, it is always cool when I discover new places, people, and things. It was early in the morning when Diddy and I arrived, so everything was quiet but when I returned to pick him up, this unassuming looking neighborhood had turned into a bustle of activity.

Carts selling Mexican corn, tacos, tamales, burritos and stews were on every corner and stores selling colorful areas rugs were on every block. People of all ages walked about their business briskly and I did not see any men loitering on corners shouting out "Loose Squares, loose squares". It was so vibrant to my eyes and it was beautiful to behold. However, on my drive home, I couldn't help but notice the drabness of the predominantly African American neighborhoods I am familiar with and couldn't help but compare them to the neighborhood I had just left behind. Like a light blub, it clicked in: the vast majority of the stores in Little Village were Mexican owned and only a pitiful few in my neighborhood and other black neighborhoods are Black owned. We as a people have gotten far away from our collective roots and it is destroying our communities.

I remember the stories my mother used to tell me about coming to Chicago during the 1940s to attend high school and the various Black owned businesses that were abundant on the South Side. I used to marvel at her because by the time I had arrived, only a fraction of those stores were still open and by the time I had arrived at teen hood, those stores were relics of the past, boarded up in shame.

These days, instead of opening businesses, some black folks, not all would rather invest their monies in over-priced clothing that will soon be out of vogue, chintzy jewelry that is also over-priced, and cars that are wrecked quickly due to drunkenness. These statements I am espousing are not stereotypical prater but actual real life experiences of people I know personally who wasted several thousands of dollars, inherited and earned on stuff that cannot make more money.

In a time when the African American unemployment rate hovers over 15 percent, it is time to invest our monies into businesses that will sustain our communities. We can not depend on the largesse of others but need to depend on ourselves. If I can manage to save some money, I would like to start a bookstore that caters to needs of Africans and African Americans since most bookstores only have a minuscule section dedicated to books of Africans and African Americans. I would not only sell books but CDs, coffee, pastries and African art. This bookstore will eventually be located in every city throughout urban America and would become renowned as centers for the African and African American Diaspora and if Borders can do it, so can I.

Our communities are missing that sense of vibrancy that I noticed in Little Village. Our neighborhoods have lost its flavor and we need it back if we are to succeed in today's society. Collective Roots is coming to America as soon as I find a job, save some money and get my credit score up. Watch out.

Great African Civilizations

There have been many misconceptions about the lives of Africans before the advent of European and American colonization. According to some historians, Africans were nothing more than savages whose only contributions to the world were farming and slaves. This is not true. The history of ancient Africa is just as interesting, complex, and sophisticated as any other ancient civilization, yet almost without exception; it is only Egypt that receives any consideration at all when writing history. Because of this mentality, European and American historians have long espoused that Africa and its inhabitants had no culture or history of their own, except what was given to them by outside factors.

However, long before the colonization of Europeans, Africans built kingdoms and monuments that rivaled any European monarchy. Nevertheless, because of racial prejudice, much of African history has been distorted and ignored to give justification to the enslavement of millions for financial profit. This paper will be discussing the ancient African kingdoms of Meroë, Ghana, and the Swahili and their rich contributions to the pages of history.

The kingdom of Meroë started around 1000 BC when Nubian rulers built up a politically independent state known to the Egyptians as Kush. Eventually, the rulers of Kush would move to Nubia and establish the kingdom of Meroë (Davis & Gates, p. 30). These rulers established their capital at Meroë around 300 B.C., and the kingdom lasted there for more than nine centuries. However, some historians feel that because Meroitic culture imitated the Egyptian culture so closely, the Meroitës brought no culture of their own to the pages of history. This is not true. According to archaeological evidence discovered in North Sudan that is over 2,500 years old, there was an old civilization along the Nile River at lower and Upper Nubia (modern day Sudan) that was older than the civilizations in the North (Egypt). Also, there is evidence that proves that the known Old Egyptian Civilization was an advanced stage of an even older civilization located in the Sudan (Davis & Gates, p. 35).

This evidence proves that Meroë had a culture and history that was even older than of the Egyptians. If anything, Egypt was a carbon copy of Meroë. This kingdom also had its own language. Most historians however, attributed their language and alphabet system to the Egyptians. It was a common belief that ancient Black Africans could not and did not develop a written language. However, inscriptions in a distinct indigenous alphabet appear in Meroë as early as the 2nd century B.C, proving that these assumptions are not true (Davis & Gates, p. 110).

This written Meroitic language was used into the 5th century, when Old Nubian eventually replaced it. Widespread use of Meroitic on monuments indicates that a significant percentage of the population was able to read it. However, the meanings of these inscriptions remain unknown, as this hieroglyphic-derived script is as yet untranslatable.

Another little known fact about the Meroitës is that they had a unusually high number of queens who ruled without male intervention. One queen, Queen Amanirenus led her army against a Roman invasion in 24 BC. She won the first battle, and despite losing a second battle, the Romans had enough, agreed to a truce and went back to Rome. Rome never did conquer Meroë, and this kingdom continued to thrive for another 200 years. Actually "queendom" would be more accurate, since the leader of Meroë was usually a warrior queen, called a "kandake" which means "queen mother" or more simply "gore"meaning "ruler"(Fairservis. p.60).

In terms of economics, Meroë was famed for its massive iron production, the first large-scale industry of its kind in the Nile Valley and had extensive trade with Greece and Rome. Because of the production of iron, the armies had better weapons to use during battle and the farmers had better axes and hoes to work their lands. Meroitë traders exported ivory, leopard skins, ostrich feathers, ebony, and gold and soon gained direct access to the expanding trade of the Red Sea (Shillington, p. 40).

The kingdom of Meroë eventually went into decline. Causes for the decline of the Meroitic Kingdom are still largely unknown. The Meroitic kingdom faced formidable competition because of the expansion of Axum, a powerful Abyssinian state in modern Ethiopia to the east. About A.D. 350, an Axumite army captured and destroyed Meroe city, ending the kingdom's independent existence.

The West African Empire of Ghana is another kingdom whose history was downplayed and attributed to outside factors. Although the Berbers originally founded Ghana in the fifth century, it was built on the southern edge of Berber populations. In time, the land became dominated by the Soninke, a Mande speaking people who lived in the region bordering the Sahara (McKissack & McKissack, p. 112). They built their capital city, Kumbi Saleh, right on the edge of the Sahara and the city quickly became the center of the Trans-Saharan trade routes.

Ghana accumulated great wealth because of the Trans-Saharan trade routes. This wealth made it possible for Ghana to conquer local chieftaincies and demand tribute from these subordinate states. This tribute, however, paled next to the wealth generated by the commerce of goods that passed from western Africa east to Egypt and the Middle East. This trade primarily involved gold, salt, and copper (Koslow, p. 70).

A hereditary king called the Ghana ruled Ghana. The kingship was matrilineal (as were all Sahelian monarchies to follow); the king's sister provided the heir to the throne (McKissack & McKissack, p. 115). In addition to military power, the king appears to have been the supreme judge of the kingdom.

Although northern African had been dominated by the religion of Islam since the eighth century, the kingdom of Ghana never converted (McKissack & McKissack, p. 120). The Ghanaian court, however, allowed Muslims to settle in the cities and even encouraged Muslim specialists to help the royal court administer the government and advice on legal matters.
The original founders of Ghana ultimately proved to be its demise. Unlike the Ghanaians, the Berbers, now calling themselves Almoravids, fervently converted to Islam and in 1075, declared a holy war, or jihad, against the kingdom of Ghana. Little is known about what exactly happened but nonetheless, Ghana ceased to be a commercial or military power after 1100. The Almoravid revolution ultimately ended the reign of Ghana.

Europeans and Arabs alike have portrayed the history of the Swahili kingdom as one of Muslim-Arab domination, with the African people and its rulers playing a passive role in the process. However, recent archaeological evidence found shows that the Swahili people are descendants of the Bantu speaking people who settled along the East African coast in the first millennium (Horton & Middleton, p. 70). Although both Arabians and Persians intermarried with the Swahili, neither of these cultures had anything to do with the establishment of Swahili civilization. These cultures became absorbed into an already flourishing African civilization founded by ancient Bantu Africans.

The eastern coast of Africa changed profoundly around the close of the first millennium AD. During this time, Bantu-speaking Africans from the interior migrated and settled along the coast from Kenya to South Africa. Next, merchants and traders from the Muslim world realized the strategic importance of the east coast of Africa for commercial traffic and began to settle there (Horton & Middleton, p. 72).

Marriage between the Bantu women and men of the Middle East created and cemented a rich Swahili culture, fusing religion, agricultural architecture, textiles, food, as well as purchasing power. From 900 A.D., the east coast of Africa saw an influx of Shirazi Arabs from the Persian Gulf and even small settlements of Indians. The Arabs called this region al-Zanj, "The Blacks," and the coastal areas slowly came under the control of Muslim merchants from Arabia and Persia (Horton & Middleton, p. 75). By the 1300's, the major east African ports from Mombaza in the north to Sofala in the south had become thoroughly Islamic cities and cultural centers.

The language that grew out of this civilization is one of the most common and widespread of the lingua franca: a lingua franca is a secondary language that is a combination of two or more languages. Swahili or Kiswahili comes from the Arabic word sawahil, which means, "coast." Swahili belongs to the Sabaki subgroup of the Northeastern coast Bantu languages. It is closely related to the Miji Kenda group of languages, Pokomo and Ngazija (Horton & Middleton, p.110). Over at least a thousand years of intense and varied interaction with the Middle East has given Swahili a rich infusion of loanwords from a wide assortment of languages. Even with the substantial number of Arabic loanwords present in Swahili, the language is in fact, Bantu.

The Swahili civilization expanded southwards until they reached Kilwa in Zanzibar (from the Arabic word al-Zan). Later, its inhabitants carved out a small territory even further south around Sofala in Zimbabwe (Horton & Middleton, p. 140). While the northern cities remained localized and had little influence on African culture inland from the coast, the Sofalans actively went inland and spread Islam and Islamic culture deep in African territory (Horton & Middleton, p. 150).

The major Swahili city-states were Mogadishu, Barawa, Mombasa (Kenya), Gedi, Pate, Malindi, Zanzibar, Kilwa, and Sofala in the far south (Horton & Middleton, p. 155). Kilwa was the most famous of these city-states and was particularly wealthy because it controlled the southern port of Sofala, which had access to the gold, produced in the interior (near "Great Zimbabwe"), and its location as the farthest point south at which ships from India could hope to sail and return in a single monsoon season.

These city-states were very cosmopolitan for their time and they were all politically independent of one another. In fact, they were more like competitive companies or corporations, each vying for the lion's share of African trade. The chief export was ivory, sandalwood, ebony, and gold. Textiles from India and porcelain from China were also brought by Arab traders (Horton & Middleton, p. 175). While the Arabs and Persians played a role in the growth of the Swahili civilization, the nobility was of African descent and they ran the city-states (Horton & Middleton p.195). However, the nobility were Muslims and it was the Muslims who controlled the wealth. Below the nobility were the commoners and the resident foreigners who made up a large part of the citizenry.

However, Islam itself penetrated very little into the interior among the hunters, pastoralists, and farmers. Even the areas of the coast near the trading towns remained relatively unaffected (Horton & Middleton p.198). In the towns, the mud and thatch houses of the non-Muslim common people surrounded the stone and coral buildings of the Muslim elite, and it seems that most followers of Islam were wealthy, not poor.

Still, a culture developed for the Swahili that fused African and Islamic elements. Family lineage, for example, was traced both through the maternal line, which controlled property, an African practice, and through the paternal line, which was the Muslim tradition. Swahili culture had a strong Islamic influence but retained many of its African origins.

These city-states began to decline in the sixteenth century; the advent of Portuguese trade disrupted the old trade routes and made the Swahili commercial centers obsolete. The Portuguese wanted native Africans to have no share in African trade and busily set about conquering the Islamic city-states along the eastern coast (Horton & Middleton, p.225). In the late seventeenth century, the imam (religious leader) of Oman drove the Portuguese from the coast, and gradually established his authority over the coast.

The existence of these ancient African civilizations proves once and for all that Africa had a culture and a history of its own other than Egyptian that endured for centuries before the advent of outside factors. The kingdom of Meroë ruled for centuries before the Egyptians and deserves its rightful place as one of the premier ancient civilizations of the world.

The kingdom of Ghana proved that Africans were capable of managing their own affairs without the intervention of Europeans. The Swahili and their language were around for centuries before Arabians and others "discovered" them. These civilizations had their own culture, language and commerce before the advent of Europeans and Muslims in Africa and for the most part, the world does not know anything about them. That is a major crime against the study of history and hopefully, through more archaeological studies and writings, the rich and interesting history of these magnificent civilizations will be told and treasured for future generations.

Pickin' Greens with My Momma on Sundays

Dear Ma,

Although you have been gone out of my life for five years, you are never far away from my thoughts. Instead of being weepy when I think about you, I have decided to concentrate on my wonderful memories of being a little girl who was so spoiled and pampered that I did not realize how poor our family really was until I got older. I never did without and I will always honor you for being the type of mother who made things happen against great odds.

My fondest memory of us is pickin' greens with you on Sundays. Cooking a large Sunday dinner for your family was a tradition you brought with you from Mississippi and you used to throw down!! On Sundays, you and I would go to the local corner grocery store and you would choose your items carefully. More often than not, chicken would be the meat dish because it was delicious and cheap. The same for greens and you would get the salt pork or the ham hocks, to season up the greens. I used to beg you to make Kraft Macaroni & Cheese just so I could lick the can.

Your favorite greens were a combination of mustards and turnips with turnip bottoms thrown in for added flavor. I can clearly see myself standing next to you in the kitchen helping you pick the greens while you told me stories of hants and skeletons that would not stay still to entertain me and to keep me moving. I used to play with the leftover stems, pretending that I was cooking Sunday dinner for my Barbies and depending on your mood, you would either make hot water corn bread, fried on the stove or you would bake the corn bread in the oven. I used to love when you made crackling bread smothered in butter.

WGN Channel 9's Sunday Matinee would be in the background and the house smelled deliciously of fried chicken, greens, and love. Sometimes relatives and friends would drop through and discuss everything from politics to relationships. You and Cousin Cleo thought ya'll was slick, spelling out words to try to keep me from understanding ya'll conversations. I used to memorize the letters and went into the next room to write them down. I was always a smart one.

I am so happy to have these memories of you to sustain me on these cold winter nights when life can look so bleak. When I am filled with despair about my job situation, I can think about you, the strongest woman I know to this day and know that my time is coming. You came up here from Berclair, Mississippi, a town so small I can barely find information about it on the Internet, to Chicago as a teenage girl to attend George Washington Carver High School in 1948 and you made a life for yourself in a city where only the strong survive. You were a sharecropper's daughter who picked cotton as a little girl younger than your youngest granddaughter and I am so proud that your blood flows in my veins.

Well, Ma I have to say goodbye for now but not forever. As long as I have my memories, I have you. Remember, in June, we have a graduation to attend. Your Nu-Nu is coming out of college! I am cooking the soul food celebration of the Millennium in honor of your granddaughter and you because without you, there would be no Kathy, Noelle, Anthony or India and I love you for that.

Love Always,
Your Daughter Kathy

Tales of a Little Ghetto Girl

I was the youngest of three children born in 1970 to my mother. She was a single mother long before it became the norm and I think it was very brave of her to the make the decision to bring life into the world instead of having a back alley abortion because she was not married. I have two siblings, two brothers, one of whom is now deceased. I did not feel bad because my father did not live in our household but I know that my brothers were affected by not having a father. Both of them used to rage against my mother for being "bastards" and mentioned this fact frequently during family fights.

My view on the "bastard" situation was that regardless of the fact that our father was not around, our mother was. She worked at a series of low-wage paying jobs to keep a roof over our heads, clothes on our backs, and food on the table and my brothers should have been more grateful. I have friends who will not provide even the most basic needs for their children so I will be forever grateful for my mother's diligence and would never disrespect her or her memory because my father was not around.

My mother was everything to me. My first memory of her is when I was about two-years-old. There was a horror show called "Creature Features" that aired during the seventies, and I remember running to my mother when the music for the show came on because it was so scary to my two-year-old self. I knew that she would protect me from those scary creatures because she was my mommy and mommies are supposed to protect their children.

Our relationship was close until the day she died. I never left home: When I got my own apartment, she moved with me because I could not imagine my life without her. I remember being a little girl and listening to stories about her life as the daughter of two sharecroppers, picking cotton in the fields of Itta Bena, Mississippi. My mother passed on December 6, 2006 and life for me will never be the same. I will always remember her touch, her skin, her smell.

When adolescence came, things got crazy. I turned from a bookworm into a hot mama and subsequently became pregnant at fifteen. Ma never told me that she was disappointed in me but realistically, I know she was both hurt and angry. I was a good student up until high school and the pregnancy. I graduated in the top ten when I was in grade school and I was expected to go places and do big things and she knew that an adolescent pregnancy would set me back in life and it did. I eventually dropped out of high school but I will get to that later.

At one time, I had two older brothers named Randy and Larry. Randy was the middle child and he died on February 7, 1994, his thirty-fourth birthday from a drug overdose. He was a victim of the crack epidemic of the eighties and he was lost to me and my family from the moment he started using drugs and I miss him. Randy was a homosexual also. I believe that was one of the reasons he turned to drugs because it could not have been easy to have been black, male and homosexual during the seventies and eighties when he came of age.

He was born in 1960 and he was fun, if albeit mean at times. Younger siblings are great targets for the older ones and he could be a jerk but his generous, loving nature is what I remember best. He would press and curl my hair and turn me into a diva. I was a doll lover when I was little girl and he brought one of my favorites, an 18 inch doll named Candy and she came with makeup and hair dye. I loved to make up her face and color her hair.

He started out smoking marijuana and progressed to powder cocaine and then to crack. I know all of this because I spent a lot of time with him between the ages of ten and thirteen. He never did drugs in front of me but when he had company, I heard conversations between him and his friends. I was not the tattle-tale type of sibling so he trusted me to keep his secrets. My fondest memory of him is him taking me to the Jackson Victory tour at Comisky Park in 1984. He was a big fan of Michael Jackson but I was crazy about that brother and really believed that he was going to be my future husband. Randy gave me one of my fondest childhood memories and made it possible for me to be the envy of my friends.

My other brother Larry is fifty-five and an alcoholic. He was born in 1956 and has been an alcoholic for most of his adult life and it saddens me. We were not as close as Randy and me but I love him. He got married at an early age because his girlfriend was pregnant and he did not want his child to be a "bastard" like him. He had two children, Latonya and Latamara. Latamara died at the age of two due to suspicious circumstances: scalded with hot water. If her death had occurred today, Beverly, Larry's ex would be serving time for murder and child abuse. It happened in 1978 and I really do not know the real story but I know that my brother has been drinking ever since she died.

He is a semi-functional alcoholic who managed to work but not for long because of his disease. I remember when Randy got him a job setting up banquets at the Art Institute of Chicago where he worked and Larry got fired for stealing alcohol on the job. Randy was furious to say the least and their relationship eroded and was never the same. It makes me sad to see my closest living blood relative outside of my children succumb to alcoholism. He has been to rehab countless times and is looking forward to death according to him. I tell him God has a different plan for him because after numerous hospitalizations, fights and cirrhosis of the liver, he is still alive.

My mother was seventh of twelve children and at one time, I had eight living aunts and three uncles. Now I have one aunt and several cousins. I grew up in a family building owned by my Aunt Maggie. She purchased a brick two flat at 7246 South University back in 1963 and my family moved in. My mother and two brothers stayed in the basement apartment, Aunt Maggie, her daughters Cleo and Kim on the first floor and Grandma, Aunt Mary, Aunt Rosie and her boyfriend Bay on the second floor. I have wonderful memories of that building growing as a child. I would go to floor to floor, receiving love and affection from everyone. Because I did not have a father, my aunts and grandmother spoiled me to death. They purchased clothes, toys, gave me money and most important, love to an inquisitive little girl. Everything changed when my Aunt Maggie was diagnosed with schizophrenia and my extended family broke up. Although we managed to see each other on the summer holidays, the camaraderie of the old days were gone.

My mother always said that Aunt Maggie was never the same from the moment she came back from a trip to Jerusalem in 1970 and I do not know exactly what happened. Aunt Maggie was in her fifties when she was diagnosed, but if she did not take her medication, she became violent. Aunt Rosie and Aunt Mary moved out the building and my grandmother moved to Wichita, Kansas to stay with my Aunt Annabel and her family. My mother decided to stay because she did not want to leave her sister alone and we moved on the second floor.

From the moment I was born, I was surrounded by older, southern black women who took no crap from a smart-mouth chap. I was brought up to respect my elders and my grandmother carried a leather strap in her apron pocket to enforce her rules. The other women who lived on my block looked out for me as well. Older women like the ones who surrounded me during my childhood and adolescence are a dying breed of strong, sometimes flawed black women who struggled to pay the bills, raise their children and others, deal with racism, sexism, and crazy men but managed to keep their dignity. I feel sorry for children and teenagers that live in our current society because they missed out on these fabulous women.

Most of my "mothers" are now gone; my own mother, almost all of my aunts except and all my other "mamas" on my old block have died except for one and that breaks my heart. When you are young and full of yourself, you do not think about these ladies until you reach an age in which your own mortality is staring you in the mirror and I wished I had took the time to sit down with these ladies to listen their knowledge and wisdom. But I am still blessed because I got my cousin Cleo.

Cleo is the second child of Aunt Maggie and she is a combination of mother and sister to me to this very day. She gave me one of my favorite books as a child "Gone With the Wind" and when she got in the car to go anywhere, I was right by her side. She fed me, pressed and curled my hair every Sunday and put up with me when I interrupted her dates with her fella, Lacy, who brought me my first bike. When I had my oldest daughter, she brought formula, diaper and clothes and treated me as if I was her child. In the past couple of years, her health has not been the greatest, having had a quadruple-bypass surgery and subsequent kidney dialysis. She is another lady in my life that I cannot imagine being without and childishly hope that she lives forever.

I was a chubby child during my childhood and I developed breasts at the age of nine. I remember my chest hurting like crazy and laying on the couch crying with my mother patting me on the back and giving me aspirin and water. She knew what was happening but I did not and before I knew it, I had grown quite a set. I had perverts following me street on foot and in cars and old men who knew my mama leering at me and offering me money. I declined all offers.

I was a bookworm when I was a child and lived in my own little world with my books and dolls. When I read "Little Women," Barbie and friends became Jo, Meg, Beth and Amy. When I read Greek mythology, my mother's old slips and nightgowns became togas and tunics sewed by me. I learned to sew during that period of childhood and loved to make doll clothes for my dolls. Having read so many books, some of them adult, it was hard for me to relate to other children and I preferred to play with my dolls. On the occasion that I decided to play with the children on the block, I was teased and sometimes had to fight.

My brothers were male and too old to help me with my battles but I had my mama, who had no problem with checking a little girl who had the nerve to touch her baby. I was called a nerd because I loved to read and all I wanted to do was fit in. Sometimes young girls can be quite catty and although I was raised around a group of women, pettiness and cattiness is not in my nature. When I became a teenager, I found some buddies and my mother said my vocabulary went down because I was hanging with "riff-raff."

I did not have a lot of friends during my childhood but I was in a clique by the time I was an adolescent. As stated earlier, I was in my own world when I was under the age of fifteen but around that time, I met my current best friend LaShonder. In some ways we were complete opposites: she was an extrovert who loves crowds and I was an introvert used to her books and fantasy land. She brought me into official teen hood by taking me the Museum of Science and Industry on Sundays where teens from all sets congregated and socialized during the mid-eighties.

My cousins Lisa and Caraline were friends of mine during this period. They were the daughters of my Aunt Blanche and mother occasionally allowed me to spend the night and we used to have a ball playing with dolls, reading raunchy romance novels and fighting with her brothers. They even found my first boyfriend, Willie, after deciding their nerdy cousin needed a man.

After Caraline got involved with a boyfriend she was dating when she was fifteen, we did not hang together as much as we did and Lisa and I become as close as blood sisters, a closeness we still share. She is a year older than I and has been one of my biggest motivators. When I dropped out of high school, she nagged me to get my GED and drove to Chicago from Detroit, Michigan on May 11, 2006 to see me walk across the stage to receive my Bachelors degree. Although we are not blood sisters, I love her like one.

My self-esteem was not the greatest during my teen years because I had a weight problem and thought that I was ugly. I knew that I was smart, but being smart in the ghetto is looked down upon and my young silly self gave into the pressure of being ignorant although I continued to read. However, although I had self-esteem problems, I had enough sense not to get involved in anything that would get me an ass-whipping. If my friends were talking about doing something stupid, I would excuse myself to a chorus of jeers.

I became pregnant with my oldest child several months before my sixteenth birthday. Becoming a teenage mother was not due to peer pressure; it was due to ignorance. I should have told my mother that I was sexually active and she would have taken me to get on some birth control but because I was so afraid of her reaction, I did nothing and ended up pregnant as a result and gained a bad reputation. I did not have sex because I was pressured into it by some horny little boy but because of natural curiosity, not understanding that curiosity combined with ignorance leads to serious consequences.

When I found out I was pregnant, I was so scared I kept it to myself for several months, not knowing that my mother immediately knew what was up because she noticed the extra clean bed sheets and no requests for sanitary napkins. I wore big clothes to hide my enlarging figure and cursed the creature that was growing inside of me. My mother eventually confronted me about the pregnancy and I broke down and cried and admitted that I was pregnant and guess what: the world did not end and my mother stood by my side.

On April 24, 1987, Noelle Dominique Henry came into my world and my life has not been the same since. Because I did not receive prenatal care until it was almost time for me to go in, I had complications due to the fact Noelle passed bowel movements while still inside me, which caused her heartbeat to go down every time I had a contraction. The doctors gave me a c-section and she came into the world weighing 6 pounds and 11 ounces.

Because she and I were both ill, I did not see her for two days but when I did, the fear and hatred of the creature who had invaded my life faded away. She was awake and she looked directly at me with an expression that said "Are you my mommy?" I fell in love with her sweet little face and all my maternal instincts kicked in. She has been a total blessing to me and I had the pleasure of seeing my baby girl walk across the stage in June 2005 to receive her high school diploma and as a member of the National Honors Society with a 4.0 grade point average.

I dropped out of school during my senior year of high school like a ninny and I will always have regrets about that decision. To this day, I cannot come up with a reasonable explanation for my one fit of insanity because I was a good student all through grade school. I was always the smart girl who read books but when I went to high school, I was one of many and that was hard for me to get used to. I received the first F's of my academic career when I was a freshman and my natural enthusiasm for learning turned sour unfortunately. Eventually, receiving an education would become a top priority for me but not until years later.

My family is fire-breathing Southern Baptists and because of that, my mother rarely went to church. I believe the hell-fire, everyone is going to hell rhetoric she heard on a regular basis when she was a child turned her off organized religion but she read her Bible religiously and could quote scriptures and made sure I went to church every Sunday until I was around thirteen. When I spent the night with Caraline and Lisa, we went to church every Sunday but my aunt changed churches frequently, so it was quite an adventure.

I believe in God but like my mother, am not particularly religious and have been called a heathen on several occasions, but I do not think of myself as a heathen but as someone who questions everything, including religion. I respect and try to adhere to moral rules of the Bible but it make me furious when people who claim they are religious get upon their moral soap boxes and spew out hatred and venom towards people not like them.

When I look around and notice the lives of some children and young adults in Chicago's ghetto, I pity them and know that my adolescence and childhood was blessed. Although I was poor in monetary goods, I never felt poor because my mother made sure I had everything I needed. I was surrounded by family who loved and petted me and I had friends. Getting pregnant at such a young age was the most traumatic experience of my childhood and subsequent adolescence because it set me back financially and I am still paying the price for my actions right now.

I did not receive my GED until I was twenty-six and graduated from college in 2006 at the ripe old age of thirty-five. Although I got laid off from my job as an administrative assistant August 2007 and have not found stable employment since then, I have enough faith in myself and in God to know that my life will turn out fine. The little girl who wanted to become the first, African American female district attorney still has a few tricks up her sleeves and will achieve all her dreams.

Searching For Assata

If asked the question, "How much would you be willing to sacrifice for your beliefs?" the average individual would probably look bewildered. Would you be willing to give up your friends, family, freedom, even possibly your life for a cause that was dear to you? The cynic inside me says, "Probably not." In this society, people have a tendency to speak with much grandiloquence about their beliefs but when asked to sacrifice for those same beliefs, they crumble. Assata Shakur did not. Assata Shakur is a revolutionary and one of the most wrongly convicted individuals in U.S. history. Her story is a sad chapter in American history, in which race, social class, political affiliation, and gender played a role in her subsequent exile from her homeland.

On May 2, 1973, racial prejudice would change the life of Assata Shakur. An incident of what would now be labeled "racial profiling" takes place on the New Jersey Turnpike. Ms. Shakur, an active participant in the Black Liberation Army (BLA), was traveling with friends, Malik Zayad Shakur and Sundiata Acoli when state troopers stopped them, reportedly because of a broken headlight. A trooper explained that they were "suspicious" because they had Vermont license plates. The three were made to exit the car with their hands up. All of a sudden, shots were fired. When it was all over, state trooper Werner Foerster and Malik Shakur were killed.

Ms. Shakur and Mr. Acoli were charged with the deaths of state trooper Foerster and Zayad Malik Shakur. While held in jail, she was shackled and chained to a bed, with bullet wounds still in her chest. She was also forced to undergo the jabs of shotgun butts of the New Jersey State troopers and heard their voices shouting Nazi slogans and threats to her life. In the history of New Jersey, never had a female prisoner ever been treated as she, confined to a men's prison and placed under a constant twenty-four hour surveillance of her most intimate bodily functions.

Ms. Shakur and Mr. Acoli were eventually sentenced to life plus thirty-three years. Although the verdict was no surprise since it was an all White jury who convicted them, many questioned the racial injustice of the trial because it was riddled with many human rights violations and constitutional errors. The pretrial publicity was extremely negative and African-Americans were purposely excluded from the jury. Even more incredible was the fact Ms. Shakur was shot with her arms in the air, making it anatomically impossible for her to commit the murders she was convicted of.

However, in the country of the United States where there is suppose to be freedom, justice, and liberty for all, the only people who have that luxury are the rich, particularly, white folks. Ms. Shakur had the triple jeopardy of being black, female, and poor and she was a member of a political organization that had been targeted by the CIA and the FBI because of its political views. Any organization that challenges the status quo has to be eliminated at all costs.

Assata Shakur spent six and a half years in prison, two of those in solitary confinement. During that time, she was beaten and tortured on a daily basis. Although there is no mention of rape, she was probably sexually harassed everyday of her imprisonment. While imprisoned, she gave birth to her daughter Kakuya, whom they took away a week after birth. On November 2, 1979, fearing for her life, she made a daring escape that continues to infuriate the United States government to this day. In 1984, she was granted political asylum by Fidel Castro, dictator of Cuba and was finally united with her daughter. On May 2, 2005, the federal government issued a statement in which they labeled Ms. Shakur a domestic terrorist. In addition to doing that, the government also increased the bounty on her head from $150,000 to an unprecedented $1,000,000.

When I first read about Ms. Shakur's story, I cried. She was a young woman like me who was shot, beaten, sexually harassed and generally treated like shit because of her race, sex, class and political affiliation. She was unjustly sentenced to jail for two murders she did not commit for these same reasons. The part that is really scary is what happened to Assata can happen to me, my daughter and any other black woman in this country whom the police and the courts deem deviant. Black women have been historically stereotyped as sexually deviant troublemakers who need to be controlled.

Also, according to the Labeling Theory, groups with the power to label individuals deviant, exercise total control over what and who is considered deviant. Ms. Shakur was deemed to be deviant by the courts and the U.S. government because of her race, gender, political beliefs, and class status; therefore, she was sentenced to prison without any due process of the law. While in prison, she received horrific treatment at the hands of her jailers.

During her pregnancy, she received no prenatal care and the authorities even tried to starve her so she would miscarry. Although this type of treatment of female prisoners is extreme, most do not receive adequate medical treatment while in prison. According to research, health care in women's prisons is limited, and prenatal care is nonexistent. If pregnant, female prisoners' babies are taken right after birth. They are also treated no differently than men in prison. Ms. Shakur experienced this first hand and she was beaten everyday the six years she was in prison.

Writing these words was one of the most emotionally wrenching projects I have ever done. Reading about Ms. Shakur's experiences brought up feelings of pain and anger but my feelings are minuscule when I think about the tears that she wept and still weeps. Imagine being convicted for the murders of two people, one of them your best friend and you are innocent. Imagine your other friend being convicted of the same murders and he was innocent too. Imagine being mentally tortured, beaten, and starved for six years of your life, living in a cage. Imagine giving birth to your daughter and having her taken away a week later. Imagine escaping from prison and being exiled away from your family and friends, knowing that you might not see them or the country of your birth again.

These are things that Assata Shakur has experienced everyday of her life and knowing that makes me as guilty as the criminal system that wrongly convicted her. I am guilty because I was ignorant of her history and had forgotten about the struggles of her and other African-Americans who fought for equality in this country. This woman in essence gave up her freedom for a cause she held dear and how many people are willing to that? She was and still is, a true warrior woman in every since of the word. The only thing I can do to repay Assata and the others who have sacrificed their lives in the battle for equality is to raise my children to be strong, productive members of their race who are proud of their heritage, and not afraid to fight for their rights.

The Death of the American Dream: Poverty in America

In the United States, disparities between rich and poor have risen sharply. Low-income individuals are increasingly unlikely to escape from their economic position of poverty. There are few stories of how someone made it from "rags to riches," and poor families are increasing their annual working hours, if they have jobs. According to research, income inequality is far greater in America than in other major countries such as Great Britain, Australia, and Canada. Current statistics show that the rich is getting richer and the middle-class and working poor are being left in the dust.

Although America is thought of as the land of material wealth and success, poverty has existed persistently since it was founded. Large numbers of Americans have been and still are poor: they lack the resources to feed, clothe, and shelter themselves adequately according to socially defined standards (Rand, 2004). There are many issues when looking at poverty because it is a problem that permeates every dimension of culture and society and has different meanings. Social poverty means that some people will be denied the right to a decent education. Political poverty means that innocent people are imprisoned on the basis of their skin color and politicians turn a blind eye. Economic poverty means there will be limited employment opportunities for some and inadequate housing.

When individuals are poverty-stricken, they have to make choices between paying bills or buying school clothes and supplies for their children. When individuals are poor, their living conditions are often lacking in essentials such as gas, water, and electricity. They cannot make life or death decisions because they lack monetary and social capital. In essence, poverty is the state of living without economic, political and social resources that are necessary and requisite for achieving success in this society.

Poverty is powerlessness, a lack of representation and freedom. The only point in which individuals would not be considered poverty-stricken is when there is a fundamental change in the distribution of goods and services in American society and everyone is on a more equal playing field. In the United States, poverty can be defined either as biological, meaning that individuals cannot meet biological needs and relative, which describes a person as poor in comparison to other members of their society (Iceland, 2003).

The Census Bureau measures poverty by using a set of money income thresholds that is based on the family's size and structure. If a family's income falls below that particular threshold, they are considered poor. These thresholds consist of money income before taxes such as work earnings, public assistance, alimony, child support, social security benefits, and trusts. There has been much criticism of the way the Census Bureau measures poverty because it is considered archaic and miscalculated. The most important aspect used to measure whether an individual is living below the poverty line is income.

According to the Census Bureau, only cash income is considered in a family's income, not the other types of government assistance such as Food Stamps, school lunch programs and earned income tax credits. A family of four with three children under the age 18 would be considered poverty-stricken if their total income falls below $19, 233. In Chicago, as many as 253,000 more Chicago residents -- 87,000 of them children -- are likely to have been pushed into poverty as a result of the recession, according to the Heartland Alliance Mid-America Institute on Poverty's newly released 2009 Report on Chicago Region Poverty. The projected increase would represent a 27 percent jump in the number of people living in poverty in the state over the past two years.

My definition of poverty is quite different than the one used by the Census Bureau and OMB because I measured not only economic resources, but political and social. The Census and the OMB only measures cash income. The definition used by the Census and the OMB do not allow for constructs such as social and political deprivation. The individuals who use this definition obviously do not understand that being impoverished is more than lacking money.

Poverty is a state of mind that causes people fall behind academically, to be more likely to commit criminal acts, and to lose hope. Poverty not only decimates pocketbooks but spirits. There are several ways that poverty might be conceptualized. In 2002, the Census Bureau compared a set of alternative measures designed by the National Academy of Sciences with its own official measure. However, the findings were mixed. Under a set of alternative measures that added non-cash benefits, the poverty rate increased. That is why the Census Bureau uses its official measure. The United States wants to pretend that poverty does not exist and if it does, only a few are actually afflicted, usually people of color.

The existence of poverty in America is a complex situation and so are the solutions necessary to correct it. Huge campaign contributions from large corporations and wealthy individuals dominate politics, economics, and social policies in this country. The needs of the poor are not on the agendas of these individuals. Because of those in power, there are conservative government policies that undermine helping the disadvantaged and pad the pockets of the privileged. The various debates on whether the official measure of poverty is correct are stupid and do not change this fact: America has forgotten about a certain segment of people based on their economic background.

Some have argued that the rate economic growth has been insufficient to eliminate poverty, whereas others maintain that the cause is because of an unequal distribution of income. Some see the poor as lacking the skills or the will to escape their condition; others see the economy as dependent upon the poor to provide a low-wage labor force for various industries. This lack of agreement has long been characteristic of public disagreement about poverty. As long as American society is one of conflict between the classes, nothing will change.

Not the Average American Family

My family would not be considered "normal" by societal standards because I am an unmarried African American single mother. I have three children and I have been a parent since I was sixteen. I was not trying to become a single parent at the age of sixteen but I did and there is no use over crying over spilt milk as the old folks would say. Hell, I have been called "Momma" for so long that when I am in a grocery store and hear a child say "Momma", I automatically look around, even though my children are at home.

I think that I have been a good mother but Lord knows I am not perfect. I was just a child when I had my eldest daughter and if it was not for my mother; God knows what would have happened to me and my baby girl. I eventually had two more children and my little family of four means everything to me.

I love when we have family meetings in my bedroom discussing everything from politics to Facebook drama. All of my children are opinionated as hell and I love it because you cannot be a wimp in this society because people will step on you like a cockroach.

As a single mother, I had the pleasure of seeing my eldest children walk across the stage as high school graduates. I take pride in those accomplishments because according statistics, children of teen mothers will drop out of school, start breeding the next generation of bastard children, and become natural born killers. Not true at all; it depends on the teen mother. I would never sit back passively and allow my children to become statistics of the streets.

My first little birdie flew the coop two years ago and has her own apartment and I am so proud of her. She has been working since she was fifteen-years-old and she has more work ethic than some forty somethings I know. She managed to keep a 4.0 in high school while working a part-time job and when she graduated, she was a member of the National Honor Society. She recently graduated from Robert Morris University in June of this year and is planning on pursuing a Master's Degree in Information Technology. That's my Nu-Nu.

My son is a remarkable young man. He has never caused me a moment of grief since he was born. I am one of the few mothers in the inner-city who can say emphatically that my son is a good kid. At an age when most young men are hanging out on street corners, he picks his little sister up from school. This marvelous child of mine elected not to go on prom on the premise that he was not interested in "girlie" stuff like that, but I think he did not go because my financial situation.

My little one is my clinger. She refuses to sleep by herself and insists on sleeping with me. She rubs on my rolls and tells me to never lose weight because my fat is soft and warm. She says my Afro is a beautiful cloud and that I am the most beautiful mommy in the world. She loves me unconditionally and wholeheartedly and my life would be so empty with her.

As stated earlier, I did not plan on becoming a single mother but I love my children and as long as my children are alive and breathing, I would do anything for them. They are the best part of me and I have no regrets.

The Original Feminista – Ida B. Wells-Barnett

Ida B. Wells-Barnett was a short, feisty little black chick from a small town in Mississippi who, with the written word, managed to punch a powerful hole into the prevalent mainstream white male ideologies of her time.

She was born Ida Bell Wells on July 16, 1862, in Holly Springs, Mississippi. It was the second year of the Civil War and she was born to a slave family. Her mother, Lizzie Warrenton, was a cook; and her father, James, was a carpenter. Ida's parents believed that education was very important and after the Civil War, they enrolled their children in Rust College, the local school set up by the Freedmen's Aid Society (Hine 1993). Founded in 1866, the Society established schools and colleges for recently freed slaves in the South, and it was at Rust College that Ida learned to read and write.

Her life changed forever the summer she turned sixteen. Both of her parents and her infant brother died during a yellow fever epidemic, and Ida was left to care for her remaining five siblings. She began teaching at a rural school for $25 a month and, a year later, took a position in Memphis, Tennessee in the city's segregated black schools.

Upon arriving in Memphis, she learned that the teaching salaries were higher than Mississippi. She also found out that even though there was a stronger demand for literate individuals to teach, there was a stronger need for qualified ones. According to Salley (1993), because she needed qualifications in order to teach, she made the decision to enroll into Fisk University and gained her qualification in under a year. While returning to Memphis from a teaching convention in New York, she was met with racial provocation for the first time while traveling by railway. Ida was asked by the conductor to move to the segregated car, even though she had paid for a ticket in the ladies coach car.

She refused to leave; biting the conductor's hand as he forcibly pushed her from the railway car. She sued the Chesapeake and Ohio Railroad, and was awarded $500 by a local court. Although she won the case, the headlines read, "DARKY DAMSEL GETS DAMAGES," and the decision was appealed to the Tennessee Supreme Court and was reversed (Bolden, 1996). She was ordered to pay court frees in the amount of $200. This incident infuriated Ida and spurred her to investigate and report other incidents of racism. Outraged by the inequality of back and white schools in Memphis and the unfairness of Jim Crow segregation, Ida became a community activist and began writing articles calling attention to the plight of African Americans.

She wrote for a weekly black newspaper called The Living Way. Her teaching career ended upon her "dismissal in 1891 for protesting about the conditions in Black schools" (Salley 115). During her time as a school teacher, Wells-Barnett along with other black teachers was said to have gathered and "shared writing and discussion on Friday evening, and produced a newspaper covering the week's events and gossip." (Lengermann and Niebrugge-Brantley 151).

The newspaper was officially established and was published and distributed under the name Memphis Free Speech and Headlights and it was distributed throughout the black community a year after she was dismissed. It has been said that her motivation to become a social analyst was the results of her involvement with the Memphis Free Speech and Headlights both as editor and columnist under the pen name Lola and as part owner. However, her printing press was destroyed and she was run out of town by a White mob who went crazy with the idea of a Black woman having enough moxie to stand up for her people.

After getting dismissed from her teaching position, her attention shifted from schools to the issue that would dominate her work for most of her life; lynching. Lynching was the brutal and lawless killing of Black men and women, often falsely accused of crimes, and usually perpetrated by sizable violent mobs of Whites.

After the Civil War, black men made immediate civil rights gains such as voting, holding public office, and owning land and some whites were infuriated with their success and groups like the Ku Klux Klan were established. They made it difficult for Southern Blacks to vote or live in peace, attempting to maintain white supremacy through coercion and violence, including lynching (Salzman, 2004). Infuriated by the Memphis lynching in 1892, which involved a close friend, Ida expressed her grief in an editorial: "The city of Memphis has demonstrated that neither character nor standing avails the Negro if he dares to protect himself against the White man or become his rival. There is nothing we can do about the lynching now, as we are outnumbered and without arms. There is therefore only one thing left we can do; save our money and leave a town which will neither protect our lives and property, nor give us a fair trial in the courts, when accused by White persons" (Hine, 1993).

At the same time Wells saw what lynching really was; an excuse to "keep the nigger down" and execute blacks "who acquired wealth and property." (Duster, 1971). Since whites could no longer enslave blacks, they found in mob violence a different means of maintaining a system of "economic, psychological, and sexual exploitation" (Duster, 1971). In addition, the result of her investigation and editorial sparked the Black community to retaliate against lynchings and encouraged blacks to move if they could and those who stayed to boycott the city Railroad Company, which was done with much success. Ida saw the success of the boycott, and asserted, "The appeal to the white man's pocket has ever been more effectual than all appeals ever made to his conscience." (Duster, 1971.)

She used an amazingly straight-forward writing style to prove a very bold argument against lynching, discrediting the excuse of rape and other excuses. Wells used specific examples and sociological theories to disprove the justifications of lynching made by Southerners. Within her pamphlets, Wells portrays the views of African-Americans in the 1890s. Southerners allowed widespread lynchings while hiding behind the excuse of "defending the honor of its women."(Jones-Royster, 1997).

The charge of rape was used in many cases to lynch innocent African-American men. The victim's innocence was often proved after his death. Wells asserted that the raping of White women by Negro men was an outright lie and supported her statements with several real stories about mutual relationships between White women and Black men and the hypocrisy of White men who had relationships with Black women, but would kill Black men for the same thing. As shown by Wells, the excuses used by Whites to torture and murder blacks were false.

After the Civil War, Whites could no longer depend on black slave labor for their livelihood. When African Americans were slaves, they were considered "property" and "obviously, it was more profitable to sell slaves than to kill them"(Jones-Royster, 1997). With all restraint of "property and profit" lifted since the slaves were now free, Whites during and after Reconstruction were able to freely give into their anger and hate by torturing and killing blacks.

Wells' investigations revealed that regardless of whether one was poor and jobless or middle-class, educated, and successful, all blacks were vulnerable to lynching. Black women, too, were victimized by mob violence and terror. Occasionally they were lynched for alleged crimes and insults, but more often black women were left behind as survivors of those lynched. Up to this time, Blacks had almost never been free from some form of persecution; the period of Reconstruction was particularly difficult. With the occurrences of lynching steadily increasing with no hope of relenting, their new found freedom ensured little safety.

Eventually, Wells was drawn to Chicago in 1893 to protest the racism of the exclusion of African Americans from the World's Fair. With the help of Frederick Douglass, she distributed 20,000 pamphlets entitled "The Reason Why the Colored American is not in the Columbian Exposition." At the age of 33, on June 27, 1895, she married Ferdinand Lee Barnett, lawyer and editor of the Chicago Conservator, and continued to write while raising four children with him (Duster, 1971). Ida believed firmly in the power of the vote to effect change for African-American men and women.

She saw enfranchisement as the key to reform and equality, and she integrated the Women's Suffrage movement by marching in the 1913 Suffrage Parade in Washington, D.C., with the all White Illinois delegation (Sterling, 1979). She continued to write in her later years, and remained one of the most widely syndicated black columnists in America. She published articles on race issues and injustices that were printed in African-American newspapers nationwide.

Toward the end of her life, Ida worked to address the social and political concerns of African-Americans in Chicago. She made an unsuccessful run as an independent candidate for the Illinois State Senate in 1930, and died the next year of the kidney disease uremia (Duster, 1971). Wells-Barnett's influence was profound. When the federal government built the first low-income housing project in Chicago's "Black belt" in 1940, it was named in her honor (Sterling, 1979). Her autobiography was published posthumously by her daughter, Alfreda Duster in 1971.

In Chicago, she helped to found a number of black female and reform organizations, such as the Ida B. Wells Club, the Alpha Suffrage Club of Chicago, and the Chicago Negro Fellowship League. She also served as director of Chicago's Cook County League of Women's Clubs. These clubs were a means for blacks to join together for support and to organize to effect change (Duster, 1971). At the national level, Wells-Barnett was a central figure in the founding of the National Association of Colored Women, a visible organization that worked for adequate child care, job training, and wage equity, as well as against lynching and transportation segregation.

Ida B. Wells-Barnett's passion for justice made her a tireless crusader for the rights of African Americans and women. She was a social reformer, a suffragist, a civil rights activist, and a philanthropist, wife, and mother. Her writings, regardless of the risk to her safety and life, raised public awareness and involvement to address a number of social ills resulting in the oppression or murder of African Americans. Her service of time through the creation of myriad clubs and organizations improved the lives of her people. Her work in Chicago, in her final years, focused on providing for the needs of the city's African American population. Modeled after Jane Addams' Settlement House efforts, Wells created urban houses for black men, where they could live safely and have access to recreational amusements while they searched for employment (Hines, 1993).

Ida B. Wells-Barnett is sometimes referred to as the "Mother of the Civil Rights movement." She refused to be moved from the Whites only railway car eighty years before Rosa Parks held her seat on an Alabama bus. She encouraged the black community to take steps to gain political rights, using the same means that would successfully be used much later during the Civil Rights movement such as economic and transportation boycotts (Hines, 1993).

In similar fashion to Margaret Sanger (of the birth control movement) and Susan B. Anthony (of the Women's Suffrage movement), Wells-Barnett was a woman who dedicated her entire life to upholding her firm beliefs about social reform. She began by writing about the disparity in education and school conditions for black children and spent much of her life working to abolish lynching through public awareness (Hines, 1993). Ida, through her writings, public speaking, and service in various organizations, elevated the voice of women's equality and suffrage. She was a pioneering black female journalist, and led a very public life in a time when most women, black or white, did not actively participate in the male political realm.

Ida B. Wells-Barnett was connected to many prominent leaders and reformers, male and female, during her lifetime. Among them: Jane Addams (1860-1935) was a social reformer, social worker and the founder of Chicago's Hull House, the most famous of the settlement houses. Addams and Wells-Barnett successfully worked together to block the segregation of Chicago's public schools (Sterling, 1979). She was also connected to W.E.B. Dubois (1868-1963) a famous black scholar, sociologist, researcher, writer, and civil rights activist who voiced opposition to the accommodationist views of his contemporary, Booker T. Washington (1856-1915). Washington urged African Americans to focus on self-improvement through education and economic opportunity instead of pressing Whites for political rights.

Ida B. Wells outwardly disagreed with Booker T. Washington's position on industrial education and was mortified with his implication that "Blacks were illiterate and immoral, until the coming of Tuskegee." (Hine, 1993) Outraged by his remarks, she considered his rejection of a college education as a "bitter pill." (Hine, 1993). She wrote an article entitled "Booker T. Washington and His Critics" regarding industrial education. "This gospel of work is no new one for the Negro. It is the South's old slavery practice in a new dress." (Hine, 1993).

She felt that focusing only on industrial education would limit the opportunities of aspiring young Blacks and she saw Washington as no better than the Whites that justified their actions through lynching. Wells-Barnett joined Dubois in his belief that African-Americans should militantly demand civil rights, and the two worked together on several occasions, most substantially as co-founders of the NAACP. The National Association for the Advancement of Colored People (NAACP), of which Ida B. Wells-Barnett was a founding member, is still a thriving organization with thousands of members nationwide (Hines, 1993). The association continues to advocate and litigate for civil rights for African Americans.

Two of the primary issues on which Wells-Barnett worked on, anti-lynching and women's suffrage, are now defunct issues. Lynching is a federal crime and women received the vote in 1920 with the passage of the Nineteenth Amendment to the Constitution. For this reason, related groups that arose at the time, such as the Anti-lynching League, the Freedmen's Aid Society, and the National Association of Colored Women are no longer in existence. Yet, the League of Women Voters was created as an outgrowth of the suffragist movement, and is an organization that still educates men and women about their responsibilities as voters.

Wells-Barnett's contribution to the field of sociology is so significant that her work "predates or is contemporaneous with the now canonized contributions of White male thinkers like Emile Durkheim, Max Weber, George Simmel, and George Herbert Mead, as well as the contributions of White female sociologists like Adams, Gilman, Marianne Weber, Webb, and the Chicago Women" (Lengerman and Niebrugge-Brantley 171). Ms. Wells-Barnett is an inspiring example of the power of the written word and the determination to succeed despite the odds.

She was an African American woman, the daughter of slaves and considered the lowest of the low on the historical totem pole in American society and her tenacity, ambition, courage and desire for justice changed history. She was direct and possessed strength during a time when this was unheard of by a woman, especially a Black woman. A reformer of her time, she believed African-Americans had to organize themselves and fight for their independence against white oppression. She roused the White South to bitter defense and began the awakening of the conscience of a nation.

Through her campaign, writings, and agitation she raised crucial questions about the future of Back Americans. Today African-Americans do not rally against oppression like those that came before. Gone are the days when Black folks organized together; today Blacks do not want to get involved as a whole unless it personally benefits them. What this generation fails to realize is that although the days of Jim Crow have disappeared, it is important to realize that the fight for equality is never over. In the preface of On Lynching: Southern Horrors, A Red Record and A Mob Rule in New Orleans (a compilation of her major works), she writes, "The Afro-American is not a bestial race. If this work can contribute in any way toward proving this, and at the same time arouse the conscience of the American people to a demand for justice to every citizen, and punishment by law for the lawless, I shall feel I have done my race a service. Other considerations are of minor importance" (Wells, 1969).

America's Issue with Black Women
One of the hardest jobs in the world is to be a black woman. We do not get paid our worth and are generally treated like shit. Some might disagree with this premise but I bet my last pair of draws that whoever disagrees with me is not a black woman. It seems like no matter how much we achieve, it is never good enough. Even with a black First Lady in the White House, in the past couple of years, black women have been relentlessly attacked for their looks (average looking Asian man writes an article on the undesirability of black women and gets famous), their educational aspirations (how dare you black bitch have the nerve to get educated!), mothering skills or lack there of (black women either have more children out of wedlock and or more abortions than any other racial group according to whatever new group with an agenda comes out) and we cannot get a break.

From the moment we were brought to this country as broodmares, we have been used up and tossed aside like trash by not only the majority but our own people. Some of our men have taken to the Internet to discuss how trifling and unattractive black women are without realizing that every time they open their mouths; they are talking about their mommas. Some of our women, trying to curry favor with black men, will diss a black woman from the top of her head to the tips of her toes, even her own black daughter to look good in their eyes, not understanding that they are black women too.

From the moment a little black baby girl is born, her psyche will be inundated with negative stereotypes about black women. She will grow up hearing about the exploits of Sapphire, Mammy, and Jezebel who are the older sisters of Skeezer, Bust-Down, Hood-Rat, Gold-Digger, Baby Momma, Welfare Queen, and Crack Whore. She will learn that the life of a little black girl means nothing and that is she goes missing or dies, the media will not pay attention and her body might not be found for months, if ever. She will be told that she is an ugly, fat, nappy headed bitch and to go sit down in a corner somewhere until someone decides to fuck her. Due to this "you ain't shit" brainwashing, some of our little girls grow up believing that the only thing they have of value in this world is their sexuality.

Unfortunately, this is the life of a black woman in America but do not count us out yet. We have survived the hell of having our children sold off on the action block, watching our men get hanged in trees and getting beaten within an inch of our lives while fighting for basic civil rights and still we rise. Every person on this planet owes his or her existence to a black woman: Mitochondrial Eve. So when society feels the need to degrade and devalue the existence of black women and you are a black woman, tell society to kiss your entire ass.

Not Just Another Welfare Queen

I did not plan to become a parent at sixteen and it has not been easy, emotionally or financially, but I do not have any regrets. Being a mother is the greatest role in my life. People have no idea how difficult and all-consuming being a parent is, particularly, a single, poor one. The right wing and the media have been in cahoots for decades in their efforts to stigmatize African American single mothers as lazy, unstable and responsible for passing on a culture of poverty from one generation to the next and those stereotypes are not true.

What is true is that African American mothers in this country have juggled work and children for decades before it became socially acceptable, sometime neglecting their own physical and mental health in order to keep their children clothed, housed and fed. Although I do not have material wealth to spend on my children, I love them fiercely and am doing my best to raise them to be strong, productive members of society. As a mother, that is the least I can do.

I have always used welfare as a revolving unemployment office: on welfare when not working, no welfare when working. I had worked in the clerical/administrative field during the late nineties, during the Clinton administration, and jobs in my field were plentiful. From 1992 to 1998, I did temp work and it was great! As soon as one position ended, I would go to another, often at a higher pay. In 1998, I found full-time employment and that job lasted for a year but I had to leave due to a single mother's worst fear: babysitting problems. After that, I went back to temporary employment from March of 2000 to October of 2000. I was fired from that job because I was pregnant and the temporary agency I worked for did not want put up with someone who would have to take off days for prenatal appointments-- another obstacle single mothers have to put up with in the working world.

By that time, our current President was in office and the economic system had totally changed. My days of making between 9 and 12 dollars an hour (big money for welfare recipients) were a done deal. The only job I could find between 2000 and 2002 was a part-time administrative assistant position. The pay rate was not bad, but I only worked twenty-five hours per week and there were no benefits because it was a part-time position. In addition, the recruiter that hired me lied about my job duties. I was under the impression that I would be using my word processing skills and would be busy. What I was actually hired for was to be a fax checker/relief receptionist. For six hour a day, I would check the two fax machines in the office and make copies of the material that came in. I also distributed mail into the mailboxes of everyone in the company. At the end of the week, I would throw away the junk mail and mail out anything important.

Checking those faxes and dumping that mail really got on my nerves. Why couldn't those lazy, overpaid executive check their own mail? And the mail! It amazed me that people would come to work everyday and did not check their mailboxes. These executives had the audacity to complain when the boxes go full. If you could notice that your mailbox was full, what was so hard about taking the mail out? I actually threw away magazines out of spite. It was a waste of postage and time. No wonder that so many corporation end up filing for bankruptcy with all the waste that goes on. The only good thing about the job was the reception part.

After working there a week, I was told that my job was a dead end situation, meaning there was no opportunity for advancement. Even if I worked like a slave, there would be no raises, no growth, nada. All of the other administrative positions were filled and those women were not going anywhere. Any job posting were for people who had degrees and I did not have one. The people at my company, particularly the women, made me feel like I was nothing because I did not have a degree. I was truly on the low end of the company totem pole. When I asked for extra work, I would be given papers to shuffle. How boring is that? It was no wonder that my attitude towards this job started to stink very badly.

I knew my days at this company were coming to an end when I saw another woman being interviewed. Even though I might have been wrong, she did not look as though she had a degree either. Two days later, I was let go by my supervisor, who was very nice about the situation. She explained that this was not her decision but others at this company did not think I was a good fit for the position. I know she was wondering why I did not look sad because I was being fired, but I did not shed a tear and I took my severance check and got the hell out of there.

A month later, I was on the system once again. This time, I had to go to a work program because of my prior work experience, which I did not have a problem with. I needed a job, but this particular program was designed by idiots. The first day of training, the trainees were instructed to use crayons and paper to draw a shield and put our job and life aspirations in the shield. I could not believe this crap. How would this aid welfare recipient in obtaining a job? This program is what welfare reform and the taxpayers are paying for-- training grown women to use crayons.

After doing this program for two weeks, I received papers that I did not think I would ever get. Earlier that spring, I had applied for a loan consolidation for student loans I had taken out during my turbulent teens when I wanted to become everything from a beautician to a security guard. Since I had heard nothing from the U.S. Department of Education, I forgot about it. When I read the papers, I was told that I was no longer on default, my loans were consolidated and I was eligible for financial aid. Thank you God! I was going back to school and to hell with that stupid program.

Immediately, I went to Chicago State University, started the registration process and was accepted in less than a month. I was so proud of myself. I called my caseworker at the job program and told her my plans and she did not have a problem with it. However, my caseworker at the welfare office was a major obstacle to my collegiate career. She told me that since I had work experience, they would not allow me, a grown woman, to go to a four-year college. The most I could do was a two-year program, majoring in medical assisting or obtaining some more secretarial skills. I was so angry, I cried. How could these people who did not know me, tell me what was best for me? It was the beginning of a three and half year war with the caseworkers of the Woodlawn Department of Human Services for my right to attend college unimpeded.

Battle one: The first problem I had was the massive turnover of caseworkers who were assigned to me. Every time I went to the office, I had a new caseworker who would send out mixed messages. One caseworker would have a problem with my decision to attend college without permission, the next one would not, and my TANF case got totally messed up as a result. This fact would turn out to be a major turning point in my war with the welfare system.

Battle two: after finally being assigned a steady caseworker, who at first seemed like she was down for welfare recipients receiving an education, turned out to be a witch of the first degree. She wanted me to come into the office every other week to let her know how I was doing. Although I was not working, I was in school full-time taking fifteen to eighteen credit hours per semester, raising three children in the ghetto, coping with my elderly mother who is not in the best of health, and dealing with being flat broke with children. I felt that coming into the office every other week was too extreme and made my thoughts known. I was quickly "sanctioned" thereafter. Getting sanctioned means that your cash benefits are slashed in half until whatever issue your caseworker has with you is resolved.

Imagine a check for $435 a month being cut to two-hundred seventeen dollars and fifty cent and being expected to live off that. I had to make choices between paying my bills and buying clothes for my two younger children for three months. Thank goodness that my eldest daughter had a part-time job and I had Section 8 housing, or I would have gone crazy.

Battle three: Eventually my caseworker and I came to an agreement and I started receiving my full benefits again. But just when I thought the drama had ended, the harassment about me being in college full-time and not attending a welfare job program began. Even after maintaining a 3.75 grade point average, I was still pursued by the welfare system like the Furies of Greek mythology for trying to improve my human capital. Eventually I made the decision to not get cash benefits, only food stamps. I was hoping that the two years of college I had obtained would make it easier for me find employment but the only job I found was college-work study. I could not work more than fifteen hours per week and it was minimum wage. I was broke as hell and going crazy: I even thought about giving my children to the state until I could get myself together financially.

But, I got over that madness quickly. However poor I was, these were my children and we were going to ride out the storm. I should not have had children until I was financially secure but they were here now and they were mine. There is no one in the world more fit to raise my children than myself, however poverty-stricken I was. I swallowed my pride and went back to the welfare office to apply for cash assistance in June of 2003 and never heard another word from them for almost three months. I eventually contacted a sociology professor of mine from the previous semester, Professor Judith Birgen to see if she knew anyone who could help me with my welfare situation. She put me into contact with Diane Doherty, Executive Director of the Illinois Hunger Coalition, who in turn put me into contact with a lawyer with the Public Aid benefits legal hotline.

To this day, I do not know what this lawyer said to my caseworker and her manager, but I received my cash benefits within three days and an abundance of food stamps. I had never felt so empowered in my life! I knew then that even welfare recipients had basic rights and that my rights were being violated by the Woodlawn office. Welfare recipients are treated like "riff-raff" and little information is given or spoken to them of their rights. Little did I know that a major battle with welfare was brewing and the war to receive a college degree was just heating up.

Battle four: In January of 2005, I made the decision to transfer from Chicago State for two reasons: I was bored with the curriculum and the administrative system was insane. I decided to apply to Roosevelt because of its reputation and because Harold Washington graduated from there. I figured that any college that produced an intelligent, articulate individual such as the late mayor Harold Washington was a college I needed to attend.

In March, I was notified of my acceptance into Roosevelt and was delighted to find out that I received a recognition scholarship for my previous academic excellence at another school. I also received a letter from the Roosevelt Scholars program, encouraging me to apply and I did and was accepted on another scholarship! I was flying high for the first time in my life: In making the decision to attend college, I found out that I was so much more than a "welfare recipient." The professors at Chicago State and Roosevelt University thought that I was an intelligent, articulate person who was capable of obtaining a Bachelor's degree. Too bad Public Aid did not care and still continued its harassment.

In September of 2005, my caseworker had the audacity to cop an attitude because I did not inform her that I was transferring to Roosevelt. I was a grown woman who was making a decision about my life that I thought would be best for me and I was not about to answer to her or anyone else. The Personal Responsibility contract clearly states that recipients can go to school and if attending, must maintain a 2.75 grade point average. But caseworkers and their managers are more consumed with pushing welfare recipients into the workforce, although some of those jobs pay minimum wage, have terrible hours for mothers and have no opportunity for growth. She took issue with the fact that I registered for day classes because according to her, I was suppose to register for evening classes and go to a job training program in the day.

I looked at this woman as if she was insane. Yeah, I was broke as hell but I was not going to stand for any interference when it came to my collegiate career. My grade point average was over the average mandated by the welfare system and if necessary, I would call legal assistance. While meeting with her and the manager, I also learned that my TANF clock was at 57 months, which meant that I had only had 3 months left to receive cash assistance.

As of February of 2006, I would only receive food stamps and no cash. I immediately informed them that my clock was at 37 months when I went to college and my estimation was 48 months. Welfare recipients who are in school must wait until they receive their first grades before the clock actually stops and registering for school does not stop the clock. One would think that the my caseworker would know this since she had been my caseworker for almost two years, but caseworkers are some of the most clueless creatures on the planet. Dealing with people who are poor, uneducated, and sometimes ignorant cannot be easy for caseworkers but they should not take it out on the recipients are trying to do the right thing.

I was scheduled for another meeting because my caseworker and her manager needed to investigate my case further and I was to come back in two weeks. During the appointment, I was verbally harassed about my decision to attend college, was told that I should have done it sooner, that I had no business attending Roosevelt University without their permission and so on. I could not believe the nerve of these harpies.

I know women who register for school just to receive a babysitting check and some who would not attend school if offered money was offered in the millions and these individuals had the nerve to be on my case for attending college and achieving? The world is full of hateful, mean-spirited people and I had the misfortune to be in the company of two of them. I did not lose my cool though; I just sat there and listened to their nonsense because I did not want to go to jail for acting crazy. Nothing or no one was going to stop me from obtaining a college degree. I knew I had basic rights as a welfare recipient, however little, and that I needed to develop a counterattack as soon as possible because this war was getting crazy.

Resolution: When I got back from the welfare office, I checked my mail and there was a letter from the Springfield office where Public Aid in Illinois was headquartered and was given the same information that my caseworker and my manager had previously informed me about. However, I did not know that I could file for a 6- month extension for good causes. I filled out the paperwork for that and I also wrote a letter to Springfield, explaining to them my situation and discussing the negligence of the Woodlawn Office to keep track of their recipients' records. I did not want an extension; I just wanted my clock readjusted so I could graduate in May, find a job and finally be financially independent. I dropped the letter in the mail and waited.

In November of 2006, I received a letter from my caseworker, informing me that if I did not graduate and be working in my field of study by May of 2006, I would have to attend a mandatory job training program. I knew then that I had won the war and little to my surprise; I received a letter from Springfield later that week, informing me that I would not receive an extension because my TANF clock had been readjusted to 48 months, the exact amount I had calculated.

I beat the welfare system, a system that punishes it recipients for being poor and unmarried! Kathy Maria Henry, teenage mother, high school dropout and welfare recipient, had the power to move Springfield into making a decision that would benefit her life. I now had an opportunity to finish out my senior year of college in peace without welfare breathing down my neck. I beat the welfare system at their own game and it felt so good!

However, this was only the beginning of a tide of good fortune for me: in February of 2006, I was offered full-time employment at Ketchum Directory Advertising with complete life, health, vision, and dental benefits, paid time off, holidays, making $25,000 a year as a Group Administrative Assistant and I accepted. That salary might not be a lot to some, but this amount enabled me to leave the welfare system for good and be officially over the poverty line. I also graduated from Roosevelt University on May 12, 2006, graduating with honors and as a member of the Franklin Honor Society.

Writing this paper has been a catharsis for me and it allowed me to finally let go of the anger, helplessness, and the resentment that I had bottled up inside of me for the past four years. The main lesson that I learned as a welfare recipient is that even the lowliest have rights and that dreams can come true. My dream of obtaining higher education that would enable me to earn a decent living wage to support my children and I have been fulfilled and I know now that I can achieve anything that I want in life.

My eldest child graduated from high school in June of 2005 and she is attending Northern Illinois University on a partial scholarship! I kicked all those statistics in the butt! I am living proof that a single, poor, Black mother can successfully raise intelligent, productive children while receiving welfare assistance. I do not know what the future holds for my youngest two children but with God on my side and the self-perseverance that has been a key ingredient of my character; I hope to start a Henry tradition of everyone attending and finishing college. My children know of my struggles and I hope that they look at those struggles as a life lesson: never give up.

The Legend of Sweetie Mae Brown – The Baddest Bitch in Town

In spite of her name, Sweetie Mae Brown was the meanest woman in Sugar Shack, Mississippi. She was big as a linebacker. She once picked Scooter Davis, who was six feet tall and at least 250 up by the back of his neck like a mother cat would do to one of her kittens, and tossed him off her porch. She had beaten up on her last three husbands and was currently scouting for number four.

The men in town lived in fear that she would put her roving eye upon them. The women in town gave her a wide berth because she had accused them of wanting her husbands when she had them. Yeah, Sweetie Mae was a mean one. Mothers would use her name as a threat to keep wayward children in line. The religious would do the cross when she walked passed them. She lived in a raggedly shack on Dead End Lane. It didn't matter how hard the sun was shining in town, there was no light on Dead End Lane.

Spooky looking trees surrounded her house and seemed to reach out and grab at you if you had the misfortune to walk pass. No one wanted to tangle with old Sweet Mae. Every night, she would leave her shack and go to one the local juke joints and get her drink on. Her favorite drink was Jack Daniel's, no chaser. After slugging down a few rounds, drunk and ignorant, she would proceed to harass anyone who took her fancy.

One night it was poor Charlie Jones, whose only crime was to politely decline her request for a dance. Before Charlie knew what hit him, she had him trussed up like a hog for the slaughtering. Tossing him over her back, she threw him into the garbage can in the back of the joint. Everyone stared and then started drinking. Nobody in his or her right mind tangled with Sweetie Mae when she was drunk. They had come to think of Sweetie Mae as the nightly entertainment. Yes, this how Sweetie Mae rolled. She terrorized the citizens of Sugar Shack like this on a regular basis until the night she meet her match.

It was a typical night at Papa Charlie's Bar & Grill, her favorite joint and Sweetie had just downed a pint of Jack Daniel's when a stranger walked in. She was a pretty, petite thing with big brown eyes and a confident attitude so she immediately took everyone's attention when she walked in and sat down. Especially Sweetie Mae. She hated women like her, with her womanly ways and little body. How dared she come in her spot and take the spotlight!

With Sweetie's eye on her, the young lady sat down. A gentleman asked her if she wanted to dance. Since he was a cutie, she said yes, and to the small cramped dance floor they went. Sweetie Mae's eyes got big. That broad was dancing with Cletus Taylor, her future husband! Of course, Cletus had no clue about this, but it didn't matter. She had marked him as her own and for that, that chick was about to get beat down! They were getting their dance on something serious when Sweetie Mae came up behind the girl, grabbing her by the arm. "Look little girl, this is my man and no one messes with Sweetie Mae Brown's man!" she snarled down at the girl. There was complete silence in the bar. Cletus didn't say a word. He didn't want to be trussed up like poor Charlie. To everyone's amazement, petite drew herself up and snapped back,

"He told me he didn't have no woman, and I know a man-looking broad like you is not his woman!" The crowd watched in silent, thrilled amazement. Petite had game! Sweetie Mae's mouth fell open. She couldn't believe this little sawed off broad was talking crazy to her, Sweetie Mae Brown, the meanest chick in town.

With a quick move of her hand, she slapped the girl, knocking her against the bar. With only survival on her mind, the girl grabbed the nearest bar stool and started to beat the hell out of Sweetie like she stole her last pair of panties. Old Sweetie was laid out on the floor, with drool running out her mouth. Making her way to the entrance, the girl ran out and jumped in her car, speeding off into the night, never understanding the magnitude of what happened. The patrons of the bar cheered like crazy. Sweetie Mae had finally gotten her ass kicked! Sweetie Mae slowly got up from the floor, tears of humiliation running down her face. Oh the shame of it all! Her butt kicked by a girl who was five feet tall and a hundred pounds soaking wet! She would never live it down! She slunk from the bar, with her head hanging down, never to be seen by the citizens of Sugar Shack again.

Around The Way Girl

Everyone thought she was a stupid, uneducated slut. She didn't finish high school or have a job and her only occupation in life was a different man every day and night of the week. Not quite good enough for the local boys to bring home to mama, but good enough to screw. Not good enough for the stuck up little broads in the 'hood to be friends with, but good enough to call over to someone's porch to find out some local gossip. Yeah, everyone thought she was stupid. But she had them all fooled. No one suspected she was leading a double life.

Normally, she would play the role of the ignorant hood-rat with nothing on her mind but a high and a new man but for the last two weeks, it had been different. She had put on her longest dress, pulled her hair back in a neat bun, and she went to church. The first time, she was there for bible study; this time, revival week. While there, she would allow herself be swept up into the drama of it all and she would stand up in front of the church members to declare her sinfulness to the world, begging for someone to rescue her from her this life of depravity. Ironically, it would be some righteous man, a god fearing man who saw that beneath the long dress was a body that was full, voluptuous, and needed to be touched. He would pretend that he wanted to help this poor, misguided young woman. There would be the conversation, the sweet nothings in her ear:

"Everything is going to be okay baby. Now that you are here in the house of the Lord, He will make it better. All you need is the love of a good man and everything will be just fine."

She would smile sweetly and look up at him as if he was her reason for being alive. Still looking at him, she would say, "I walked here because I didn't have any money for carfare; could you give me a ride?" Naturally, he said yes.

How could he resist such a young tender girl with eyes that were so beseeching but yet so inviting? Of course she would have to meet him on the next block, couldn't have the hens of the church clucking. Always the same behavior, just dressed a little bit nicer. She used the same routine the last time. Amazing how gullible men could be.

On the ride home, she would act like it so hot to her. She needed some air and would ask could they go to the beach. It was so emotionally draining, telling all her sordid secrets to all those people and some fresh air would feel good. Naturally, he was down with that. It was in the fall and not too many people would be there.

At the beach, she would talk about the series of disappointments that had been her short life. The mother who showered her with love and affection, until she reached an age in which her mother saw her as a predator looking for the same prey: men. The father who was gone so long she could not remember his face. Her mother's husband who took away her innocence and left her with self-loathing and sexual knowledge too much for her to understand.

She would also talk about the men who made her feel like a queen at night, but would not speak to her in the daytime. The girls with the fake cheerleader smiles and serpent-like personalities. The school system which had no time for disturbed little girls who need nurturing, not more emphasis on state wide test scores. Then the tears would pour, real tears of pain, over the half-life she had been leading on this planet.

Always the arm going around her shoulder, the accidental, on purpose brushing of her breast, the awkward first kiss. She would let the kiss deepen to get things going. Slowly they would fall into the sand, and by careful maneuvering, she would end up on top. She would make him feel so good, so great for that moment. Then, with a quick, savage movement, she would slash his throat deeply. There wouldn't be time for a struggle, his basic instinct for survival being thwarted by his sexual need. He never saw the tiny switchblade that she hid in her hair, the hair she had loosened from the bun she wore earlier. He never saw the look of calculation in her eyes because he was too busy looking at other things.

Afterwards, she would watch him for a few minutes, making sure he was dead. Then she would drag his body towards her car, the car her victims did not know she had and had hid near the area where she would make her kill. She deliberately went to this part of the beach because it was very secluded. She would take the towels and blanket out of the trunk and with care, cleaned the blood from his body.

Unruffled by the night, she rolled his body into the blanket. With a strength most people had grossly underestimated, she put the body in the trunk of her car, closed it, rinsed her hands off, got in her car and drove away. She went to the outskirts of town, and dumped his body there, into a shallow grave she dug earlier. The other time, she used the city dump.

Last week was the first time she had killed someone. She did it the first time just to see if she could actually kill someone in cold blood. Everyone thought she was such a dumb, pathetic, excuse for a human with the intelligence of a slug. To kill, one had to be cold-blooded, methodological, concise, and cunning. No one knew about the deep-rooted resentment and hatred lurking in her heart. No one cared.

Of course, her heart was cold. Her own mother pretended to love her until her natural jealousy of other women turned her against her own flesh and blood. She knew dude was screwing her daughter. She just didn't care; she was too busy getting drunk and trying to hang on to her trifling husband. She felt the girl brought it on herself, walking around with her breasts bouncing everywhere.

The girls in the neighborhood felt the same way. The girl was the first to develop, with a cute face - they hated her for that. The boys were always skinning and grinning in her face, although they talked about her like a dog to them. What was so special about her anyway? Bitch.
And men! From the moment she developed, they wouldn't leave her alone. Her perverted stepfather who had warped her sexuality before she even had the chance to warp it herself. He even had the audacity to be a deacon at a church! The boys in the 'hood who pretended they liked her but only wanted some sex, and wouldn't even acknowledge her if it was daytime.

Especially, these last two self-righteous, piece of shits she found in the church. Going around pretending as if they really gave a fuck about her. Just like her stepfather. Ha! What a joke. They deserved to die. Going to church with their wives and families, pretending they were so holier than thou and then using the church as a trick service. It made the decision to kill men such them so much easier.

The ability to kill had given her a thrill and a thirst. Next time, she would have to change her routine. People might catch on. No, of course not. Everyone thought she was so stupid. She had killed twice and hadn't been caught. They had better watch out. She was out there.

Realizations

Have you ever had a day where it was so much drama and bullshit in it that you said to yourself, "I have had enough of this shit, it is time for a new life?" Well for me today was that day and finally, I was going to make some big time changes. But before I go into gory detail, let me introduce myself. My name is Classy Jones and I am a somewhat well-adjusted thirty year old female and mother of two. I make a nice living as a legal secretary at one of Chicago's most prestigious law firms, Goldman & Davis. I live in a nicely furnished townhouse on the South Side of Chicago, and I have a nice car. My children are two girls, ages thirteen and eleven, and they are beautiful and intelligent. I am currently reeling from the defection of their father, a pompous twit, and because of this, is currently not dealing with anyone else. From the outside looking in, I have the perfect life. Teenage mother beats the odds and did not become another statistic and is living the Black American Dream. In reality, I am seething with frustration and if I do not do something about it, I will end up in Tinley Park's Mental Institution.

My main frustrations in life are The Twit and my job. First, let me explain about The Twit. The Twit is father of my children, whom I gave fourteen years of my life to. I refuse to refer to him by his name; he does not deserve that kind of respect. I know I sound bitter, but how would you feel if you stood by a man when he was broke as hell, listened to all his dreams, put up with his drama, had his children because you knew he would be somebody one day and because you loved him only to have him run off with some floozy because she had her own business and could assist him in his career as a real estate broker? To top it all off, after making snide comments over the years about your gradual weight gain (after having his children), the woman he takes up with happens to shop at the same plus-size store you do, and do not use a comb?

After all the drama he has put me through, you know that he still has the nerve to tell me that he loves me? That he could never love another woman as much as he loves me? That his friend is an economic convenience? When he tells me this shit, I want to spit in his face. What kind of love is that? How can you love someone but manage to hurt and humiliate her the worst way possible? The problem is that I still love him in spite of all the pain he has put me through over the past two years, and he knows that. I would love for us to get back together and be a family. Love is not water. You can't turn it off when it is convenient. I guess if I can still feel like that about him, then he has the right to feel like that about me, but I think he just wants some sex, and is trying to suck up. Why do baby daddies feel like they have exclusive sexual rights to the mother of their children? In most cases, if they had not destroyed the relationship, they would. We are trying to have a cordial relationship because of the children, but it is hard. I do not want to become the baby mamma from hell, but I do not need his drama in my life right now. If it was not for the fact that he pays child support on a regular basis and school tuition, I would kick his ass to the curb. I am tired of putting my feelings aside for the sake of my children. When my feelings do matters?

The second frustration of my own personal Black Hole of Calcutta, Goldman & Davis. I have been there five years, and the hole gets bigger everyday. It is not easy being a secretary, regardless of the word "legal" attached to it. People think secretaries are nothing more than mindless coffee makers that shuffle papers, talk on the phone, and get to dress up everyday. Crap! You have to put up with machines who have a mind of their own, butt pinchers, not cute ones, but predominately broken down old coots who think because you are a lowly secretary, you are fair game, and the smug, smart ass attitudes of lawyers (including my boss) in the firm who think they are better than you because they have a degree from some broken down college and you don't.

People who have college degrees really burn me up with this attitude. It's not like I wasn't smart enough to go to college but having children at an early age made me get out into the work force early, and college was pushed aside. Between working retail and taking care of the kids and The Twit, I managed to take a legal secretarial class and became a Legal Secretary. I am very proud of my accomplishments. It was not easy doing this with two small children and working at the same time. But some of the comments from the lawyers at firm really make me boil.

Check this out. Earlier today at work, I was in the file room, researching some information for my boss when the two main offenders walked in, Lena Turner and Monica Davis. The chicks are some of phoniest broads around, complete with weave jobs. They are the type of chicks Biz Markie roasted in his rap, "The Vapors." They were discussing some college sorority reunion party they went to this past weekend, talking loudly, looking in my direction to see if I was listening to them. I did my best to ignore their idle chit-chatter, but the heifers had to drag me in their conversation.

"Cassie, are we disturbing you? I know you didn't attend college and I know this type of talk must really get on your nerves, "she said sweetly, but with viciousness in her voice and malice in her eyes.

I turned around glared at two harridans. What the hell did I do to deserve this type of personal persecution on a regular basis? It was days like this that made forty thousand a year, full benefits, and free parking look totally miniscule. But I could be just as vicious.

"By the way, the name is Classy, not Cassie, and no, I'm not disturbed at all. But I am disturbed by females who make a lot of money, drive nice cars, and wear Donna Karan suits everyday but can't manage to get their weave tracks tightened up on a regular basis. I didn't go to college, but I always get my hair done," I replied, smiling, running my fingers through my short, sassy do.

They both glared at me and ran out of the file room like they both had rockets up their behinds. Good. Raggedy-head broads. They both probably graduated at the bottom of their classes, and were trying to talk down to me like they were Rhode Scholars. Women can be trip.

My day got worse. Because of these remarks that I made in my own defense, I was called in a thirty minute conference with my boss, Mr. Baker, who lectured me on professionalism, courtesy to your superiors, and on and on. I sat there and steamed. What about the professionalism of these so-called lawyers at this firm? Just because I was a lowly little secretary, I was supposed to take all the crap in the world from these overpaid ninnies. But I know how to play the corporate game. After the speech, very correctly I replied, "I don't know what came over me. It won't happen again." We stood up and because he's and old fashioned type of guy, he held the door open for me, and I went back to my cubicle to steam some more about the things one has to put up with in order to make a living.

On the ride home from work, I reflected on the comments of the day. Even thought it hurt to admit this, it did irk me to hear people talk about college and the activities they experienced while there. Could it be underneath all the bravado, I was jealous that I had never furthered my education beyond a secretarial course?

Yes, I was. I had got so caught up in trying to make some money and not be on welfare, that I thought college was a dream for women in my position. I had children to support. I took the easy way out. What did it get me? I had a so-so career that could turn into more money if I got promoted to the executive secretary level but that would include more snide comments and more butt pinching from more powerful, lecherous old coots. No real sense of achievement. Just a gloried expensive secretary.

At home, I fed and bathed my children and put them to bed, basking in the love of the little people who love you just because you are their mommy and do not expect anything in return but love and perhaps some new clothes and some toys. They don't expect you to have a degree.

Later on that night, I took a bath and took stock of myself. I stared in the mirror, really seeing myself clearly for the first time in two years. I saw eyes that grown weary with resignation and defeat. I saw a mouth that used to be soft and full but was starting to turn into a long, thin, line, heavy with discontent. All of these changes would be permanent if did not do something about it.

I will not be a bitter bitch, mad at the world and drinking my sorrows away at the local bar. Tomorrow, I was going to use one of my personal days to register for some classes at Chicago State University. I was going to college at the age of thirty.

I was also going to have a talk with The Twit tomorrow also to check his ass about his wishy-washy behavior towards me. I was going to tell him if he really loved me, he would let me go and not lead me on. It is time for me to move with my life in all aspects and I was tired of him and his crap. I will not let a man drive me crazy. It does not matter if I still love him; he was never going to change. He's shacked up with some broad, and he does not want a family life with me and my children. Forget him; he is the one missing out. Deep in my heart, I know even if we got back together, it would never be the same. I will always be bitter towards him for breaking up our family in the first place. As long as the child support came on a regular basis, the rest was history. To quote a good book, "I don't know where I am going, but I am going somewhere."

10 Ways to Find Out if You Are a Brainwashed Negro

Brainwashed Negro: A Black individual who has internalized every negative stereotype about Blacks and their culture and is seething with self-hatred and low self-esteem. Usually believes that the only path to success and true happiness is to marry or assimilate into White culture, hoping to escape the sins of being born Black.

One of the biggest problems in the Black community is a lack of unity caused by years of self-hatred. Self-hatred in the Black community is due to centuries of brainwashing by the dominant culture into believing that Blacks and their contributions to mainstream society are worthless and that Blacks themselves are worthless and ugly. Self-hatred has caused some Black folks to demean themselves and other Blacks in many hurtful ways that are not productive to anyone. Here are 10 ways to find out if you as a Black person have been brainwashed by the dominant culture:

10. If you are still running around claiming that your family has "Indian Blood", particularly, Cherokee. I wonder why the only Native American tribe some Black folks can name is Cherokee, as if Iroquois, Mohicans, Seminoles and others do not exist.
9. If you believe that all Black NBA players are married to White women. 86% of married African American NBA players are married to Black women.
8. If you deny the African within by stating that your descendants are from the Caribbean. How in the hell did you think all those Black folks ended up on those islands?
7. If you believe that all White people are rich, beautiful, educated and are endowed with special magical powers.
6. If you tell a dark-skinned Black woman, "You are so pretty to be dark".
5. If you give an automatic pretty pass to light-skinned women just because they are light-skinned and have long hair.

4. If you refuse to frequent Black-owned businesses because you believe that their services are subpar as compared to White-owned businesses.

3. If you believe that "Good Hair" consists of hair that is long, flowing and silky, not kinky.

2. If you believe that all educated, wealthy Black men and women are married to people outside their race. As of 2007, only 4.6% of all married Blacks in the United States are married to a White partner or other races.

1. If you make statements such as "Black women have too many problems" or "I cannot find a Black man that is on my level" to justify dating outside your race. There is nothing wrong with interracial dating unless you are using it as a way to escape the deep psychological problems of hatred for one's race. Perhaps the problem is not Black people collectively but YOU personally and all YOUR issues and burdens of being Black in America.

A Letter From a South Side Apartment

A couple of years ago, I read Dr. Martin Luther King's A Letter from a Birmingham Jail and I was mesmerized by the passion and anger in his words and although we are in the second decade of the 21st century, his words still resonate. This letter I am writing is my tribute to him for giving his life for me and other disadvantaged and disrespected groups in America. It would sadden him to no end that nothing has really changed in American society in regards to race and economics. Perhaps one day, we will be truly free from the chains of racism and economic selfishness that enveloped America since its inception.

14 April 2012

My Dear Mr. Gingrich & Other Republican Presidential Candidates who believe that the Poor Blacks are the Scum of the Universe:

While confined in my lower class existence, I cannot help but think about the words you put into the universe about Black people who receive unemployment compensation, food stamps and other government benefits, people whose lives have been touched by the mean specter of poverty. Until recently, I was stressed out about receiving $318 per month in public assistance, so I normally would not have time to ponder on your condescending self-serving words because I was too busy trying to find a job in a dying economy but your words offended me so greatly I had to speak to you about this. Although I am now employed with a job title that is much fancier than it pays, I still cannot afford to move to a decent area because rent prices in Chicago for a three bedroom apartment would take most of my monthly salary, but a man as wealthy as yourself would not understand my dilemma. The current public discourse on the lives of poor Blacks in this country has been taken over by White, well-dressed, well-fed career politicians like yourself and I thought you needed some enlightenment.

First of all, no one wants to be poor. I know that you believe that little Black children spend their time discussing ways to be indigent and homeless by the time they are eighteen but the children I know have big plans for their future. My ten-year-old daughter's plans for the future change daily: One day she wants to be a fashion designer, the next a mad scientist who is going to take over the world. The one thing she has made clear is that she does not see motherhood in her future because in her words, "Being a mother takes too much work."

I know that you like to believe that the children of poor Blacks are a drain on society but you are so wrong. I was a teenage mother at the age of sixteen and had two children by the age of twenty-one. If one was to believe statistics on single mothers, I should have been a grandmother at thirty-two and putting money on my son's prison commissary. Not! My daughter graduated from college last year with a Bachelor's Degree in Business Administration and will be going back to school in April to purse a MBA and my son is college studying History. My children watched me work for various corporations who paid me very little money and proudly watched when I walked across the stage at the age of thirty-five to receive a Bachelor's Degree in Sociology with honors.

But I realize that you probably do not know too many Black people personally so when you chose to discuss them among your constituents, you like to use tired, worn-out stereotypes about them. According to you, Blacks have no work ethic and like taking baths in the piles of food stamps they receive. Blacks have been in this country since 1619 and still have not made any progress although White people have given them everything! What is wrong with these trifling Black people?

It is very easy for you and your kind to sprout these words, snugly enveloped in your cloak of White male privilege but what you do not realize is that although Blacks are no longer slaves, they were never made equal, financially or mentally. Throughout the years, American society had every opportunity to make amends to African-Americans by giving them same economic advantages as Whites, but it never happened because that would mean Blacks would be on the same economic playing field as Whites and that is a no-no.

It is funny how you like to blame the media for everything wrong in your world but the media in all actuality is your best friend. The media, owned by the ruling class, has played a major role in distorting views about social economics by pretending the ruling class does not exist and poor Blacks are the dregs of society. The media with its 'magic' can make the historical legacy of slavery and later Jim Crow laws vanish by pretending it is their fault that they are poor. By doing this, upper and middle-classed Americans learn to fear and loathe poor Blacks and refuse to understand the connection between systematic racism and high poverty levels among African-Americans.

The dominant culture has succeeded in making African-Americans subhuman to other groups, who passively accept these bigoted views. In your speeches and in the Republican debates, the message that you and others have given is to degenerate Black people at all costs and to keep poor working-class Whites in a constant tizzy about the so-called advantages given to them.

Mr. Gingrich, I feel sorry for you and wonder what you would do if Blacks did not exist in this country. Race and class was socially constructed for the advancement of Whites and the making up of a social class of poverty-stricken African-Americans who could be blamed for everything wrong in society. Take away the pretensions, the feelings of superiority that comes with having the "right" skin color and people like you in this society would be loss. No more scapegoats to blame and you would have to face up to the fact that you have no plans for making the economic system in America more equal. But it is easier to blame Blacks, who unlike your ancestors had no choice when they were brought to this country as chattel and broodmares to make the lives of the White ruling class easier.

Sincerely,

Kathy M. Henry

A Village Without Love: The Sad & Sorry State of the Black Community

There has been an ongoing war between the sexes in the Black community for decades and it is time for it to cease and desist because it is pathetic and the only people hurting are the children. 70% of Black children reside in a single parent household; usually the mother and Black children are highly overrepresented in the foster care system. Although Blacks are only 12.6% of the population, Black children are 41% of the foster care population and that is a damn shame.

Some of us are so busy arguing amongst ourselves and on the Internet about who is more trifling, Black men or Black women, that we have absolved ourselves of all parental and community responsibility. No one wants to look in the mirror and change themselves but would rather sit back and blame each other while making a slew of babies that will grow up confused and fucked up.

And a special message to some of my sisters: Just because you use abortion as a method of birth control does not mean you are better than the sister with four kids with four different men. Trifling is trifling and I made this point because I know of women who have had multiple abortions but will sit back and talk about another woman like a dog because she has children by different men. And brothers, I have not forgotten about y'all: if you do not want children, strap your boy up or get a vasectomy. Any man who is stupid enough to put the fate of his unborn children in the hands of a possibly unstable and vindictive woman deserves to have the child support system hounding his dumb ass for the rest of his life.

Last year, there has been a big movement in the media, encouraging Black women to date outside their race, in particular White men. It has been fascinating to read some of the comments from Black women on various websites as why they have decided to date interracially because they sound just like some of these brothers out here when they give their reasons for not dating their own kind. The generalizing and stereotyping from both sexes that takes place on these boards is sickening and although some of these folks claim to be "educated", they do not have a clue but are filled with self-hatred.

American culture is a patriarchal one in which all men, regardless of their race or ethnicity, have been socialized to believe that they are superior to women whether they will admit it or not. So if a Black woman thinks she will be escaping the sins of patriarchy by turning to another race, she needs a reality check. The same premise goes for those Black men who told themselves that if they get a White woman, they will be as good as the White man. Complete and utter bullshit. Just ask Tiger Woods and O. J. Simpson.

It is not okay for either Black men or Black women to state that they only date White people because Black folks are fucked up because this line of thinking, that White is always right is that of the Brainwashed Negro who has bought into every negative stereotype about Black culture and believe that if they immerse themselves in White culture, their lives will be better.

Not in this country of the one drop rule because if you are Black, then you are Black and will get treated accordingly.

I know this blog is everywhere but these are my thoughts. Stereotypes about Black men and women are running amok and are being perpetrated by us in ways that are killing us as a people. The Black community is on the edge of a precipice but instead of coming up with feasible solutions to the problems of a poor educational system and the high murder rate in inner-city neighborhoods, some of us would rather discuss Mary J. Blige's Burger King commercial or whether Beyonce's new daughter is real or a doll.

But all is not lost. My young male cousin is getting married this month and my best friend's stepson proposed to his girlfriend so Black Love is not dead. Although some refuse to believe it, Black people do get married on occasion and these stereotypes about how we do not get married needs to cease and desist. I know several married Black couples, Black men and women who have been married, divorced and widowed and Black men who have married Black women with a house full of kids and I live in the hood. All these stereotypes do is keep Black men and women at each others throats and our communities are on fire as a direct result. It takes a village to raise a child and what happens when the village is at war with each other? A generation of angry children without love and compassion.

Working for Pennies - The Harsh Realities of Being a Welfare Recipient

One of the biggest misconceptions in American culture is that welfare recipients are living large at the taxpayer's expense, receiving thousands of dollars per month while driving Cadillacs and other expensive cars. This myth is so not true and how do I know? Because for the past two months, I have been on welfare and let me be the one to tell you: being on public assistance sucks.

August 3, 2011 will be a day in infamy I will never forget because it was on that date that I received my last unemployment check and officially became one of the 99ers, a term for unemployed people in the United States, who have exhausted all of their unemployment benefits, including all unemployment extensions. After applying for over two thousand jobs, I found myself in the position of having to apply for Public Aid or be faced with disconnection notices and phone calls from bill collectors who cannot speak English.

If someone had asked me five years ago would I be in this position, back on welfare, I would have laughed because I went back to school and received a Bachelor's degree and people who have degrees are supposed to be protected from economic turmoil. I graduated five years ago from Roosevelt University with a Bachelor's degree in Sociology and a 3.6 grade point average and I am proud of myself for that accomplishment. I know that some folks turn their noses up at people who pursue a liberal arts degree but I learned valuable critical thinking skills, how to analyze and solve problems in a creative manner, and most importantly about social stratification and inequality and I have no regrets. I also have over ten years of transferable experience in the administrative/clerical field and an ability to work with all types, fools and all. However, even with all those wonderful qualities, I cannot find a job to save my life.

When I made the decision to apply for welfare, I tried to keep positive about my situation. Millions of Americans are suffering from either being unemployed or underemployed so at least I was not alone in my troubles. But I cannot lie: Feelings of self-loathing and inadequacy run through my veins on a daily basis and a rage is building in me. A rage against a society that tells individuals that a college degree is the path to a economic prosperity, but does not disclose how centuries of social inequality have kept and will continue to keep the best and brightest out of the workforce. A rage against rich, clueless politicians who believe people that receive unemployment and welfare benefits are sitting on their butts swigging alcohol and smoking dope. A rage against myself for waiting so long to get my life together and having to deal with the consequences of perhaps being considered passé in the workforce.

I was a teenage mother who did not get my GED until I was twenty-six and my Bachelor's degree until I was thirty-five. The entire time before both these changes took place, I was told by society that if I educated myself, I would get myself and my children out of poverty. Guess what? It did not work because I am back on welfare receiving $318 dollars per month. I did everything society told me to do and I am in the same position I was in nine years ago when I made the decision to attend college and that is a shame.

If I did not have children, there is no way in hell I would have reapplied for welfare. But when you are a mother, one has to make sacrifices, so I swallowed my pride and applied for cash benefits. By signing the Personal Responsibility contract in return for public assistance, a welfare recipient in essence signs her rights to being an adult away. Recipients must work for their cash and going to school is not an option. Yes, welfare recipients must WORK for their cash benefits. I know that people believe in the myth of women laying up on welfare, eating bon-bons and spitting out a baby every year while collecting those fat government checks but that is a load of malarkey.

On August 22, 1996 in the Rose Garden of the White House, President William Jefferson Clinton signed into law the Personal Responsibility and Work Opportunity Reconciliation Act, better known as welfare reform, dismantling the sixty-one year program of federally guaranteed cash assistance to needy families or what is known as welfare. Welfare recipients have five years to receive cash assistance and after that, it is a wrap. The debate surrounding welfare reform was dominated by white male politicians and journalists and focused predominately on minority women and their families living in poverty because minority women are the only ones in America who received Public Aid (sarcasm). Although President Clinton had the right idea, he and others did not take into account what would happen if the economy collapsed and finding a job would be the equivalency of hitting the lottery.

It burns my soul that I am back on the dole, working for $318 per month which is equal to $79.50 per week at six hours per day after everything I went through to better myself. If I refuse to go to any of the job sites my caseworker sends me to, I will be sanctioned, meaning that my monthly benefits will be cut in half to $159. So the next time, a hardworking tax payer complains about welfare recipients and how they are living good, eating lobster and shit, think about me, the college educated single mother who took care of her children, saw two of them graduate from high school, one from college, only to find herself and youngest child still poverty-stricken and broke as hell.

An Analysis of Richard Wright's Native Son

After reading Richard Wright's Native Son, one has to wonder who the ultimate victim is in a prejudiced society. The dominant group or the minority? Wright focuses on the affects of racism on the oppressors (Whites) and the oppressed (Blacks) in his novel and establishes in an ethnically prejudiced society, fear and discrimination will lead to deadly consequences. Bigger's fears of White society would lead him to accidently murder Mary Dalton, setting off a chain of events that would end with Bigger being sentenced to death for his crimes. Racism caused Bigger to have an abnormal fear of Whites and racism is the true culprit in the death of Mary Dalton.

When the topic of racism comes up, images of angry White men in hooded hats wearing white sheets, burning crosses in the yards of terrified Blacks come to mind, but it is deeper than that. According to sociologists Noel Cazenave and Darlene Alvarez Maddern, racism is defined as "...a highly organized system of 'race'-based group privilege that operates at every level of society and its held together by a sophisticated ideology of color/'race' supremacy. Racist systems include, but cannot be reduced, to racial bigotry".

Racism hierarchy in America society led to the subhuman living conditions that Bigger, his family, and other Blacks experienced during the 1930s. Bigger and his family resided in a cramped, rat-infested one room apartment in the Black Belt, a poverty stricken area of Chicago. The building was dilapidated and the family literally had to fight it out with huge rats with long, yellow fangs for space. Imagine growing up in this atmosphere with little privacy for yourself and you are a male child. It would be real easy for a young man to grow up warped living like this.

When he left the house, he did not go anywhere except to the local watering hole and the movies. Blacks were not wanted in any parts of Chicago, except for the narrow strip of land allotted to them. Apartment building, shacks for all intent and purposes looked down upon the streets in dismay, crying from neglect. Job and educational opportunities were limited, if at all. Bigger was not able to grow and thrive intellectually or economically in the atmosphere that surrounded him, and as a result, he became sullen and prone to violence.

When he went to the movies, he was bombarded with negative images of people like himself. The racism that Bigger and other Blacks faced during this time period was direct and in your face, not subtle and coded as it is today. Popular culture displayed this racism proudly through a media campaign of negative articles in magazines and newspapers, movies that displayed Blacks as half naked savages dancing around a huge, boiling pot of body parts, and advertisements in which Blacks were the employees and never the employers. Institutional racism was always at the root of this negativity and Blacks constantly viewed themselves as low-classed folks and less than human unlike Whites, who were always shown as educated, elegant, rich, and powerful. Positive Black role models during this time period were non-existent within popular culture.

These images of Black people contributed to Bigger's psychological shortcomings and caused him to become a monster. His life was narrowly defined by the boundaries that White society had imposed on him and other Blacks and he hated whites because of the power they had over him, but was fearful of them for the same reason. He hangs with a gang of misfits just like him, young, poor Black males riddled with self-loathing. They commit crimes, but only against other Blacks; the group is too afraid to rob a White man.

When the group finally decides to rob a White man, it does not work because Bigger starts a fight with one of them to disguise his fears. "Bigger was afraid of robbing a White man and he knew that Gus was afraid too…He hated Gus because he knew that Gus was afraid, as even he was; and he feared Gus because he felt that Gus would consent and then he would be compelled to go through with the robbery (25). Bigger turned his fear of Whites into a rage against Gus because Gus knew his secret: he lived constantly in fear of White society and he did not want the others to find out.

The murder of Mary Dalton came about because of fear. Bigger was so fearful of being found in Mary's bedroom by her blind mother that he accidently suffocates her in a misguided attempt to keep her from mumbling in a drunken stupor. He knew what would happen if he, a big black buck, was caught in her bedroom: cries of rape and charges of rape of a white woman would be forthcoming. After committing murder, Bigger, having killed by accident, now has to save himself. He must match his wits against the whole powerful white world, which has held him chained for all of his life, and for a time, succeeds.

Along the way, he foolishly rapes and murders his lover Bessie and is eventually caught by the police with the aid of the press. He is charged with the murders of both young women, found guilty in a swift fashion and sentenced to death just as quickly. White society can rest at ease that the great, black beast will be put to slumber for all eternity. But not the racism that created him. Bigger was an American production and centuries of slavery, Jim Crow, overt and covert racism was his ancestors.

The murder of Mary Dalton exposed a growing animosity that Bigger barely kept in check during his childhood and adolescence. White oppression cornered Bigger into a life of constant anger and restraint that he knew would ultimately explode and he gave in to the pressure. He recognized that his lack of opportunity would somehow determine his own fate. The pressure of surrendering to white power tamed his actions to a certain extent, but his yearning for liberation transcended all authority when he killed Mary and was able to hide her murder for awhile. Institutional racism was Bigger's teacher and the true murderer of Mary Dalton. After slavery was abolished in America, if whites had not created a society in which blacks were 'free' but never equal, the concept of a Bigger would not have occurred.

Black President = The Rise of the New Racists

Ever since President Obama was elected, I have noticed a lot of insanity from a certain segment of the White population. President Obama has been accused of the taking away the civil liberties of "real Americans" to not actually being an American at all but a Kenyan socialist communist fascist who is going to put White children in boot camps and indoctrinate them with all types of socialist, evil thoughts. He is also having too many barbeques and basketball tournaments in the White House with Jay-Z and Diddy and taking too much vacation time when he should be working. The most ludicrous thing he has been accused of is being an advocate of the poor (code word for Black folks).

Let me tell you one thing: having a Black president has not done shit for me (excuse the slang). As a Black person, my wallet has not gotten any fatter since his election; if anything, my pockets are lighter. Unemployment for Blacks under this presidency has risen to 16.7 percent, the highest since 1984 and I am among those who are unemployed, complete with a Bachelor's Degree. I have not had a full-time job since August 17, 2007 and these days I wonder how my bills are going to get paid since I cannot find a job and my unemployment benefits has expired.

When I see all those poor, misguided angry White people protesting against President Obama for his alleged crimes against White humanity, I snigger to myself and wonder where were all these people when President Bush passively watched from Air Force One while an entire city swam in their own shit after Hurricane Katrina hit or when Bush and his enablers started a war with an ideology (terrorism). But of course President Bush looked just like them and it was okay for him to make mistakes because they could drink a case of beer with him. The Light-Skinned Negro from Nowhere who went on to win the Presidency of the United States cannot make any mistakes or he is the worst President in the history of the United States.

It used to be a time in American history when racists were proud of their viewpoints and had no problem with admitting their racism (remember Governor Wallace?). Today's racists hide behind code words and the Internet and pretend that they are not racists. They are just honest, hard-working Americans who want their country back and are tired of Black folks receiving all the Section 8 vouchers, food stamps and welfare because they used to be slaves. Guess what clueless idiots? It is time to get a clue and take a couple of college courses in history, civics, and sociology. But to get an education is considered elitist to that ilk and that will never happen because some folks just love being ignorant. I am just waiting on the day when one of these racists will keep it real and call President Obama a nigger who has no business being in the White House with his Black wife and two Black children.

The Social Construction of Race in Western Society

In the age of the First Black President of America, racial rhetoric and hatred is running rampant on the Internet and spewed out of the mouths of politicians for political gain. However, what most people do not realize is that race is a socially constructed ideology. Race and subsequent racism was created by White Europeans and Americans in order to justify the enslavement of millions of people for profit. When people feel guilty about an action they committed, they will often try to find ways to justifying their reasons. This is what Europeans and Americans did when they decided to explain away the actions of human bondage by declaring Africans subhuman. In doing this, they changed the interpretation of history itself. A land where complex civilizations had existed for centuries was reduced to the "Dark Continent" and its people declared savages. All in the name of profit for the status quo and conversion the "natives" to Christianity. The history of Africa was rewritten to make Whites the conquerors that "civilized" the natives.

Although the concept of 'race' as a description of the physical differences that exists amongst people probably dates back to the dawn of the human species, most scholars agree that it was primarily through European colonization in the 16th to the 19th century that 'race' as a physical description emerged. It was when European colonizers, whose aim was mainly to seek out valuable primary products such as sugar, tin, rubber and human labor, came into contact with populations who looked different from them that racism became a dominant force in Western society. In order to maintain control of these populations, they were defined as inferior human beings primarily because of their different cultural practices as well as their not being White, the desired and 'normal' skin color.

However, pushing such people to the margins did not stop European and American white men from having sex with the local women producing several hues of brown folks all around the world. Thus, race as a biological factor was constructed in racism and became a major factor in racial discrimination. This ideology spread rapidly throughout Europe and beyond, spreading the doctrine of alleged racial inferiority. This ideology of racial dictatorship and hierarchy quickly took root in American society by the signing of a famous document, "The United States Constitution." This document clearly states, 'We the People of the United States.' The question proposed from this statement is: who exactly are "the People?"

It certainly was not the enslaved Africans because they were considered to be three fifths of a human being. In addition to the Constitution, the Declaration of Independence also posed many questions of racism. The Declaration of Independence was written to sever ties to a country in which people were denied their rights. However, the Constitution denied a group of people their right to pursue life, liberty, and the pursuit of happiness because of their skin color. It is obvious to see that the Constitution laid the framework for which a segregated, racial society was formed in America.

Enslaved Africans were just as human as the White men whose rights were secured through the signing of the Constitution, but their rights did not matter. Because they did not have any rights, they were forced to live in a society in which the government officials did not represent them. Equality and justice was not for all, just for wealthy, land-owning White men. The practice of discriminating on the basis of skin color was born and would be legal until the six decade of the twentieth century. Even in the new millennium, racial inequalities still plague America and until this country can admit the wrongs done to enslaved Africans, Native Americans and their ancestors, we will never be truly free.

The Old Warrior Finds a Home

This is the story about a stray cat named Beau. He lives on a block on the South Side of Chicago and he is an amazing creature with an amazing tale. Since he cannot speak, it is up to me to tell his story of survival as homeless pet and how he has beaten all the odds for a creature of his kind.

When I first met Beau about eight years ago, he had a home. He lived across the street from some friends of mine and he was so pretty to me. He was a beautiful, fat multi-colored brown, black and gray tom cat with white hair on his chest and a big fluffy tail. He reminded me so much of a cat I used to have named Big Poppa that I fell in love with him and made it my business to rub him and give him little treats every time I saw him.

Cats are very intelligent creatures that can recognize a kindred spirit. Anytime I would visit my friends, he would make his way towards me for his rubdowns and random kindness from a stranger. He was so beautiful in his heyday. Over the next eight years, life became difficult for Beau. The people who used to own him lost their home and selfishly abandoned Beau to the streets, something that humans often do to their pets. His once large frame became gaunt, his meows more timid, and pieces of his ears had been torn off during feral cat fights but he never lost his sweetness.

This little creature had managed to survive some of the worst winters I have seen in Chicago since 1979 but every spring, he would be sitting on the porch of the house he used to reside in, placid and sweet as ever. To be perfectly honest, after this past winter in Chicago when it was piles of snow almost six feet tall, I thought I would never see him again but when I visited with my friends, I saw him stretched out in the sun, still alive. It really blew my mind that after all these years, he would actually remember me but he walked up to me like it was yesterday when I first met him. I probably should have taken him in but since I have a male cat that is very territorial, it would not have been a good match. But it did not stop me from worrying about him and whether he would survive another harsh winter.

However, God looks after all his creatures, both great and small. Last Friday, I was in the neighborhood and made it my business to walk down the block where Beau would be. To my surprise and complete joy, Beau was sitting in the yard of someone's home with a flea collar around his neck and was again fat and juicy. My Beau had found a home! Someone had seen his sweetness and taken him in. He could now live out his old age in comfort with someone to love him.

As I sit here writing about Beau, I am crying. Some might think of me as a sentimental fool but I am just a person who loves cats and stories about individuals who beat the odds, even our four-legged ones. Beau, a warrior cat from the mean streets of the South Side of Chicago that according to statistics about abandoned cats should be dead, had managed to fight off the elements, feral cats and dogs, and the meanness of humans to not only survive, but thrive. This cat gives me hope for the future because if he can survive, so can I.

Makes Me Wanna Holla

Living in the inner-city will suck the joy out of life if you have the misfortune to live there. Who wouldn't be depressed about being surrounded by ignorant male youth lounging aimlessly on the corners bragging about the women they used to have, foul-mouthed, uncouth young women fighting over unemployed men, and older folks so beaten down by life that they spend their remaining days living in a bottle? Every where I go, I see desolation, grit and grime but I still manage to see beauty in my surroundings.

The beauty of seeing a grandmother taking her grandchildren to school at time when she should be chilling out somewhere in Florida but like the good solider she is, knows her duty. The beauty of watching working mothers take their daughters to work with them during the summer break from school, reminding me of the times I went to work with my mother. The beauty of the innocent faces of children, alight with the wonder and joy of being young and carefree. The sadness I feel knowing in a few years, some of these children's faces will have hardened into hate and apathy.

Urban decay is abundant in my neighborhood and several other communities throughout America. Vacant lots filled with trash and foreclosed, boarded-up properties are on every corner and one has to travel thirty blocks to find decent food to cook for your family unless you decide to settle for food markets in the area that sell rotted vegetables and fruit with no problem because no one cares.

Not the politicians who gloss over the plight of the poor people in this country and blame them for their unsavory lifestyles. Not the so-called middle-class, who are so afraid of being lumped with the poor that they have turned their backs on them and have taken on the beliefs of the oppressors instead of aiding them, not understanding that everyone in this country is one paycheck away from being in the welfare or unemployment office unless you are of the one percent that owns everything in America.

This is the reality of living in the inner-city. Although I am surrounded by some of the bleakest parts of human nature, I know that there is beauty in this world and refuse to believe otherwise. American society has all but written off the plight of the poor but they are here and not going anywhere. They are not nameless, faceless statistics. Poor Americans have the same dreams and aspirations that everyone has in this country: a chance to be a part of the American Dream where everyone has an opportunity to succeed and make a positive contribution to society. A chance to be somebody. Is that asking too much?

Collateral Damages - Living in Fear in Chicago

There is a war currently being waged in a predominately black and poverty stricken neighborhood in Chicago, Illinois named West Washington Park. The battle grounds are located between 56th and 65th street from Cottage Grove to Martin Luther King Drive. This war has not garnered much media attention except for the obligatory short paragraph in the Chicago Sun-Times and other media outlets. Last summer, several people were shot in the 6400 block of South King Drive, the block I reside on. All were under the age of 26 and all were black.

Urban terrorists have taken over inner-city minority neighborhoods in Chicago and no one is safe. It matters not if you reside in Beverly or Chatham: no family is immune from gun violence. My heart breaks for the families of who have lost loved ones to violence because I am a mother and can imagine the pain and agony they must go through on a daily basis. But I often wonder how much we as a community is responsible.

I have lived on the South Side of Chicago my entire life and I have noticed a sharp decline in values and respect amongst some blacks, particularly the younger set. I have seen children as young as 5-years-old cussing like drunken sailors while adults were in the near vicinity cheering them on. Young black adults dismiss the idea of a college education as foolishness and concern themselves with the consumption of mass goods, expensive alcohol, and having as much sex as possible. There is no respect for life and dysfunction reigns on a daily basis. Generation Crack has come of age and they are nothing nice.

When crack cocaine hit the streets of urban inner-cities, it decimated entire communities. I lost a brother to cocaine addiction and I know several families who have suffered because of crack cocaine. An entire generation of children who were born during this era is now young adults and they have not been taught anything. Momma was either on drugs or chasing behind a drug dealer and the children were left behind for the grandmothers, aunts, and the foster care systems to take care of. Fathers were too busy trying to become the next Nino Brown and have abdicated all responsibility for their offspring.

Everyday I live in fear that I will receive a phone call informing me that my children have gotten caught in the crossfire of this gangbanging nonsense. Between the hours of 2:30pm and 3:00pm Monday through Friday, I wait anxiously for my son to come back from picking his little sister up from school. He is a twenty-year-old who has not been to jail, graduated from high school on time, and who picks his little sister up from school without any prompting from me. My eleven-year-old is a smart little girl with a zest for life who loves the Disney Channel. Two children who have not had a chance to live and it would kill me if something happened to them because they had the nerve to step outside of their home. This fear that I go through on a regular basis fills me with helplessness and anger because at this time, I cannot afford to move and I am stuck living in a war zone, praying to God that my children are not victims.

My question for the day is this: when will a group of people who have survived the horrors and degradations of slavery, the failure of Reconstruction, and the dehumanization of Jim Crow segregation, and other injustices will finally take a stand and reclaim their children? Black people have gone through too much for our communities to dissolve into total anarchy. We are on point to lose an entire generation of young black males either to the jail system or the graveyard and no one gives cares. Not the politicians, not the media, not even their own people.

U Mad? America's Obsession with Being Miserable

Misery loves company is an old American idiom that has sadly become true considering the enormous amount of vitriol, malice and ignorance that is running amok in American political and cultural discourse these days. From politicians to radio shock jocks to ordinary folks, people have no problem with expressing their disdain for their fellow countrymen in mean-spirited, shallow ways and no one is safe from their ire, including children and the dead.

Although the pursuit of happiness for Americans is a Creator given right in the Declaration of Independence, I would bet my last dollar that some Americans are not happy with the state of their lives. Perhaps the 1% that owns everything in America is wallowing in glee, but your average American citizen is suffering economically and mentally and it has manifested itself in several ways. How do I know this? By perusing through the many Internet websites I read on a regular basis and skimming through the comment section. By the angry faces I see walking the streets of Chicago. By the stagnant economy that is decimating communities throughout America. Folks are losing hope for a better future for themselves and their children and they are mad as hell.

But instead of channeling their anger in a constructive manner, they blame others for their problems, usually the poor and minorities because they have a monopoly on food stamps, welfare and Section 8. Perhaps if they did not believe in those rags to rich bullshit stories in which all a person has to do is work hard, be humble and true and eventually your good works would be rewarded with great wealth and honor, they would be okay but unfortunately, living in La-La land is an everyday reality for some people. If that premise was true, there would be millionaires on every block.

But since some folks do not have any more sense than a chicken, they continue to vote against their economic interests, listening to code words such as "Welfare Queens", "Illegal Immigrants" , "Gay Marriage" and "Muslims", believing that these individuals are taking over their country, their jobs and everything else their tiny little media fried brains can think of.

In the meanwhile, the rich are laughing all the way to bank, counting their money and eating lobster and Kobe steaks while watching misguided Americans go to war against each other based on race, religion and sexual orientation.

Our politicians have sold us out to the highest bidder, our infrastructure is crumbling and our educational system is an abysmal mess, turning out students who cannot think critically for themselves or name the Vice-President of the United States. But some folks would rather eat ideology than food and the madness will continue. Americans will continue to be miserable because it easier to sit on your ass and complain than fight for what is right. The right to make a decent living wage and not have to choose between paying your rent or purchasing food for your children, the everyday reality for some Americans.

Works Cited

Fairservis, Jr., Walter A. The Ancient Kingdoms of the Nile. New York: Thomas Y. Crowell, 1962.

Davis, Lynn. Gates, Jr. Henry Louis. Wonders of the African World. New York: Random House Publishing, 1999.

Horton, Mark & Middleton, John. The Swahili: The Social Landscape of a Mercantile Society (Peoples of Africa). Malden, MA: Blackwell Publishing. 2001.

Koslow, Philip. Centuries of Greatness - The West African Kingdoms: 750-1900. London: Chelsea House Publishers, 1995.

McKissack, Patricia & Fredrick Mckissack. The Royal Kingdoms of Ghana, Mali, and Songhay - Life in Medieval Africa. New York: Henry Holt and Company, Inc., 1994.

Shillington, Kevin. History of Africa. Oxford: Macmillan Education, 1995